Samuel H. Kellogg

The Genesis and Growth of Religion

Samuel H. Kellogg

The Genesis and Growth of Religion

ISBN/EAN: 9783337168278

Printed in Europe, USA, Canada, Australia, Japan

Cover: Foto ©Lupo / pixelio.de

More available books at **www.hansebooks.com**

THE

GENESIS AND GROWTH OF RELIGION

THE L. P. STONE LECTURES FOR 1892, AT
PRINCETON THEOLOGICAL SEMINARY,
NEW JERSEY.

BY

THE REV. S. H. KELLOGG, D.D.

OF TORONTO, CANADA

AUTHOR OF "THE LIGHT OF ASIA AND THE LIGHT OF THE WORLD,"
"A GRAMMAR OF THE HINDI LANGUAGE AND
DIALECTS," ETC., ETC.

New York
MACMILLAN AND CO.
AND LONDON
1892

All rights reserved

COPYRIGHT, 1892,
BY MACMILLAN & CO.

TYPOGRAPHY BY J. S. CUSHING & CO., BOSTON, U.S.A.
PRESSWORK BY BERWICK & SMITH, BOSTON, U.S.A.

PREFACE.

THE Lectures herewith presented to the public were delivered in February, 1892, by invitation of the Faculty of the Theological Seminary in Princeton, New Jersey, to the students of that institution; and constitute the "L. P. Stone Course" for that year.

The limitation imposed by the terms of the L. P. Stone endowment, that the lectures of the course shall not exceed eight in number, made it impossible to attempt an exhaustive discussion of the question of the origin and growth of religion. Hence it seemed best to confine the course to a brief consideration of those theories regarding this subject, which appear at present to have the most extensive influence among those with whom the students in our theological schools are likely to have most to do; and, in the constructive part of the argument, to present chiefly such facts and considerations as appeared likely to be of most practical service to ministers and intelligent laymen, for the defence and confirmation of the teachings of Holy Scripture regarding the beginning and subsequent development of the religious life of man.

It may properly be remarked that Lectures III. and IV. are based upon articles of the author in review of the theories of Professor Max Müller and Mr. Herbert Spencer, which were published a few years ago in the "Bibliotheca Sacra," Oberlin, Ohio; but have been prepared in the light of and with reference to the most recent published works of the authors reviewed.

The Lectures are now published in the hope that they may be helpful to many more than the students for whom they were originally prepared.

S. H. KELLOGG.

Toronto, Canada,
  August, 1892.

TABLE OF CONTENTS.

LECTURE I.

What is Religion?

PAGES

Origin and growth of religion; importance and difficulty of the question — Difficulty of defining religion; must include atheistic faiths — Definitions of Spinoza, Kant, Fichte, Reville, Flint; of Feuerbach, Gruppe — Definitions grounding religion in feeling, as of Goethe, Teichmuller, Schleiermacher — Religion not a mere sense of dependence — Definitions centring religion in the will, as of Hegel, Caird — Max Müller's definition criticised — Definition assumed in these lectures; relates religion to the intellect; the emotions; the will — Justification of the definition 1–27

LECTURE II.

Religion and Natural Descent. Fetishism and Animism.

Naturalistic theories of origin of religion commonly assume origin of man by mere natural descent; necessitates denial of primitive monotheism — The assumption not justifiable — Testimony of Virchow; of A. R. Wallace — Proof of origin by descent not proof of origin by descent *alone* — A. R. Wallace again — Bearing of question on origin of religion — Fetishism and animism defined — Tiele's theory; primitive man regarded nature as living — Would not account for fetish-worship, only for animism — Tiele's argument criticised — Low intellectual capacity of primitive man unproved — Facts against this — Modern savages not primitive types — Proof from their languages — Admissions of Max Müller; of Herbert Spencer — Belief in a personal God coexists with animism and fetishism — Sir John Lubbock's mistake — Degree of religious development not conditioned by degree of civilization — Fetishism and animism not most common among most ancient peoples; *e.g.*, China, India, Egypt — Ideas of God, responsibility, sin, not derivable from animism or fetishism 28–63

LECTURE III.

Herbert Spencer's Ghost Theory.

Ancestor-worship the earliest form of religion — Belief in spirit and its survival after death to be accounted for — Mr. Spencer's explanation — Primitive man observed that some things had a visible and invisible state; might change their substance, and form; hence inferred a double of himself and all things — This confirmed by dreams, especially of the dead; whence survival of soul inferred; and *post mortem* reward and retribution — Idea of God evolved from idea of a ghost — The theory applied to fetish-worship; to nature-worship — Mr. Spencer's admission; modern savages not primitive, but degraded men — A dilemma; facts versus theory — Mr. Spencer's *a priori* primitive man; *a petitio principii* — His theory denies innate ideas; inadequate to account for phenomena of sin; for whole content of idea of God; as Cause;

TABLE OF CONTENTS. ix

PAGES

Moral Governor; as offended with man — Ancestor-worship not most common among lowest races — Idea of God coexists with ancestor-worship; no proof that the latter was derived from the former; witness China, India, Egypt — Mr. Spencer's argument from names for God; not sustained by facts — His appeal to the Old Testament — Conclusion 64–109

LECTURE IV.

Professor Max Müller's Theory of the Origin of Religion.

Professor Max Müller's attitude toward Christianity and the Scripture records — Makes religion to begin~~ning~~ with sense-perception of the infinite — Classification of sense-percepts; tangible, semi-tangible, intangible; the last-named the earliest deities — Primitive Indo-Aryan religion — Progress from henotheism to monotheism — Origin of religion explained by the origin of language — His argument based on erroneous definition of the infinite; on sensationalist philosophy — Senses cannot give idea of the infinite — Idea of moral obligation not derivable from observation of physical order — Sense-perception cannot originate idea of cause; of God as Moral Governor; of responsibility, sin, and guilt — Argument from history of Indo-Aryan religion inconclusive — Indo-Aryan religion not primitive — Order of religious development in India not as required by his theory — Recognition of a "Heaven-Father" earliest — "Henotheism," the first step in religious declension — Terminus of Indian development pantheism — Pantheism confounded with monotheism — Significant Hindoo appreciation of Professor Max Müller's Lectures on Religion 110–150

LECTURE V.

THE TRUE GENESIS OF RELIGION.

PAGES

Two factors in genesis of religion — The *Subjective* factor: the constitution of man's nature — Man has by nature a religious faculty — Proof in the universality of religion — Universal sense of dependence on an invisible Power — Laws of thought compel belief in unconditioned Being — Conscience constrains belief in a moral Power above man — In all this man contrasted with highest brutes — *Objection:* Many races without religion — Presumption against correctness of this assertion; often based on narrow definition of religion — Religious beliefs of savages difficult to discover — Assertion of races without religion often disproved after full information — *Objection:* Many individual atheists — Exceptions to a law do not warrant denial of a law — The *Objective* factor in genesis of religion: a revelation of God — Proof of such a revelation — Religious beliefs, spontaneous, universal, intensely strong, persistent — This not disproved, but confirmed by history of Buddhism; unaccountable if no revelation — Denial of revelation logically involves universal nescience — Revelation of God in conscience; in the mind; in the universe of matter and mind — Admission of Reville — Recapitulation 151-181

LECTURE VI.

THE DEVELOPMENT OF RELIGION. SIN AS A FACTOR.

Development in religion; not inconsistent with supernaturalism — Primitive religion elementary — Reville's misunderstanding of Christian belief on this point — The elementary not necessarily erroneous — Has monotheism been the beginning or the terminus of the development? — No "idle question" — Reville's assertion; "polytheism original" — Is this true? — Order of development from beginning not ascertainable historically — The order in historic times presumably that of prehistoric times — Argument from antecedent probability applied — Significance of phenomena of sin — Mistaken assumption that religious development has been normal; hence religious progress must have been the law — Reville's assumption — Sin involves consciousness of the morally abnormal — This assumed in all religions; a potent factor in their development; unscientific to ignore this — Sin involves religious degradation; by dulling conscience; by causing dread of God; as involving desire of what moral law forbids — Hence false conceptions of Deity; predisposition toward atheism, agnosticism, pantheism — Influence of pantheism; diminishes sinner's fear by denying holiness of God; His personality and moral government; makes sin a necessary stage in evolution — Influence of polytheism; lowers ideal of God; therewith lessens sense of moral antagonism between man and God — No tendency in sin to self-improvement, but the reverse; hence, that man, as sinful, should have ever tended by nature to religious elevation, impossible 182–202

LECTURE VII.

Historic Facts regarding the Order of Religious Development.

Coexistent polytheism and monotheism of ancient Egypt — Monotheism most prevalent at first; testimony of Rougé and Reville — Egyptian degradation of religion —

PAGES

Earliest deities of Indo-Aryans — "Henotheism" — Vedic monotheism — Development of pantheism; the Upanishads; the "Six Systems"; triumph of Vedantic pantheism — Modern Puranic Hindooism — Failure of attempts at reform — No development of monotheism in India — Hindoo testimony — Zoroastrianism — Relation to Vedic nature-worship — Persian dualism not primitive — The monotheism of the Gâthas — Zoroaster preached monotheism to idolaters — Development of Persian dualism — Modern Parseeism — Religion of primitive Babylonians — The "Magical Texts" — The "Penitential Psalms" — Growth of nature-worship — Shemitic influence — Philosophic speculations — No tendency to monotheism — Chinese religion — Worship of heaven and earth; of ancestors — Professor Legge's views — Religious attitude of Confucius; of Lao Tze — Religious beliefs of savage peoples — The Santâlis; the Kolhs; the Aimares; West African negroes; American Indians — No Indo-Germanic or Turanian people has ever shown a native tendency to monotheism — Inference as to primitive form of religion 203–247

LECTURE VIII.

SHEMITIC MONOTHEISM. CONCLUSION.

Asserted exception to the law of religious degeneration — The Shemitic race — All existing monotheism of Shemitic origin — "Monotheistic genius" of Shemites; Renan's assertion — "Did Israel produce the one God, or did the one God produce Israel?" — Original Shemitic conceptions of God; superior to those of most peoples; illustrated by names for God — Exceptions; the Egyptians; Bactrians — Religious degeneration of

PAGES

Euphrates Shemites — Primitive Arabian Sabeism; later worship of trees and stones — Mohammed's concessions to Arabian idolatry — Alleged Hebrew evolution of monotheism — Hebrew records affirm a universal tendency to forsake the one God — Patriarchal times — Israel in Egypt; in the wilderness; under the judges; under the kings — Total lapse of the ten tribes — Hebrew monotheism since Babylonian captivity; cannot be explained as a natural development; was in spite of natural tendencies — Recapitulation — Facts irreconcilable with supposition of a gradual evolution of monotheism from some other form of religious belief — Relation of historical monotheism to supernatural revelation — Conclusion . . . 248–275

THE
GENESIS AND GROWTH OF RELIGION.

LECTURE I.

WHAT IS RELIGION?

THAT the question of the origin of religion is of fundamental importance will be evident to any one who considers how profoundly and extensively the religious beliefs and practices of men have affected the historical development of the race. One may be a total disbeliever in religion, regarding it in all its forms as a baseless superstition, always evidencing a degree of intellectual immaturity or imbecility; yet the fact still remains of the almost universal prevalence of religion in all ages, and of the mighty influence which religious beliefs have had, both on individual conduct and on the history of mankind. Hence the question as to the origin of religion has ever been one of the greatest interest to every thoughtful and philosophic mind.

But the problem of ascertaining the genesis of religion, if approached only from the historic side, has proved one of the greatest difficulty. For the history of no nation reaches back to a point anywhere near the absolute beginning, either of religion, or of the human race. The earliest records show us religion prevailing in very early times as now; but those most ancient times are still far this side the beginning of religion, or of human life. Evidently the solution of the problem must be sought in some other way. Historic investigation will no doubt be useful, and is, indeed, indispensable in its place, but alone it will not suffice.

Before entering upon any examination of certain theories which have been proposed to account for the existence of religion, it is necessary, first of all, in order to clear thinking, to determine precisely what we are to understand by this term, "religion." The definition of such a familiar word might, at first, seem a sufficiently easy matter; but it is evident, from the great number and diversity of the definitions which have been given, that practically it has been found very difficult. Nor, when we observe how very numerous and how exceedingly diverse have been the manifestations of religion, can one wonder that to find a definition which should comprehend all these, has proved so hard. Most would doubtless say, at first, that religion certainly has to do with a man's relation to God, and would not object, perhaps, to such a definition as that of Seneca: "Cognoscere Deum et imitari"; or, in modern times, that of Mr. Martineau, namely: "A belief in an ever-living God, *i.e.* a Divine Mind and Will ruling the universe, and holding moral relations with mankind"; or, again, that of Professor Flint: "Religion is man's belief in a Being, or beings, mightier than himself, and inaccessible to his senses, but not indifferent to his sentiments and actions, with the feelings and practices which flow from such belief."

It is an excellence of this last definition that

it fully recognises the fact that religion is a complex experience, affecting man's whole nature, as a rational and moral agent, his intellect, emotions, and will. We must, however, regard this, in common with the other definitions mentioned, as open to the very serious objection, that inasmuch as it assumes the existence of a God or gods, it thereby excludes certain systems of belief and practice, universally regarded as religions, which yet ignore or deny the being of a God. Of such, the chief illustration, of course, is Buddhism. For by this time it should be regarded as finally demonstrated that such scholars as Professors Max Müller and Oldenberg, Sir Monier Monier-Williams, Rhys Davids, and others are right when they assure us that the original orthodox Buddhism, if it did not formally deny, yet utterly declined to recognise in any way the existence of a God, in any sense of that term. If not dogmatically atheistic, yet the whole original Buddhist system of doctrine and practice was so completely independent of any reference to a God, whether personal or impersonal, that if one could conceive that atheism should be finally demonstrated, not a proposition or a law in Buddhism would require on that account to be in the least modified. And yet, with practical unanimity, it is agreed that Buddhism must be accounted a religion; a fact which is the more significant that it is also among the most widely accepted of all religions.

It has been indeed rejoined to this, that Buddhism, nevertheless, however inconsistently, does recognise the being of a God. It is a fact that the Buddha himself is worshipped by many as a God; and that even in the earliest Buddhist authorities, the existence of the *gods* of Hindooism is taken for granted. As for the deification of the Buddha, however, it must be remembered that this did not belong to the original Buddhism, but is a very late development, which is even yet confined to the Northern school of Buddhism. The fact is indeed of great significance, in that it shows how impossible it is for a man to rest in a religion which does not present to him a personal object of worship; but shall we therefore venture to say that until the Buddha was deified there was, properly speaking, no Buddhist religion? As for the recognition of the gods of the Hindoo pantheon, which we find in the primitive Buddhism, their position in Buddhism is so different from that which they have in Hindooism, that practically they retain but the name. The idea of the dependence of man upon the real or imaginary beings regarded as gods, which is essential to the conception of deity, and is found in all polytheistic religions, is absent from the Buddhist conception of the gods and their relation to man. The gods themselves might all be left out of Buddhism, and its general character would not thereby be affected. We must therefore still insist that while Buddhism, by general consent, is judged to be a religion, it is yet wholly destitute of any recognition of a God, or of gods, as standing in any necessary relation to mankind.

But if we must then reject the definitions above specially mentioned, as too narrow, because excluding by their terms such a widely accepted religion as this, we must reject also all others, which, in like manner, either explicitly or implicitly, assume the recognition of a Deity, or of deities, as essential to religion. Such, for example, is that of Spinoza, that "religion is the love of God, founded on a knowledge of his Divine perfections"; or that of Kant, that religion essentially consists in "the recognition of our duties as Divine commandments"; or the closely similar definition of Fichte, that religion "is conscious morality; a morality which, in virtue of that consciousness, is mindful of its origin from God"; or, among the latest, that of Professor Reville, that "religion is the determination of human life by the sentiment of a bond uniting the human mind to that mysterious Mind whose domination of the world and of itself it recognises, and to whom it delights in feeling itself united." But in the orthodox Buddhism there is no recognition of a Divine Being who could give commandments, or whose will could be the origin of morality; and whereas the definition of Reville assumes both the existence of the human mind as distinct from the body, as also of a superior Mind, manifest in the world. Buddhism, formally and in explicit terms, refuses to admit the existence of either.

Without multiplying illustrations of definitions of this class, we may now glance at others which err in the opposite direction. Among the most extreme is that of Feuerbach, that religion is " man's worship of himself idealised"; the gods are " nothing but the wishes of men conceived as realised." The essence, therefore, of religion, consists in selfish desire. This thought has been elaborated by the positivist Gruppe, whose views have been set forth and effectively criticised by Professor Max Müller in his " Natural Religion."[1] Religious belief is "a doctrine professing to be able to produce union with a Being or the attainment of a state which, properly speaking, lies beyond the sphere of human striving and attainment." Not only does Gruppe deny the universality of religion, and therefore its necessity in some form, but he ventures to maintain the astounding proposition that religion is a comparatively recent invention.

[1] Op. cit. pp. 74-80.

Despite modern discoveries in Assyriology and Egyptology, he doubts if the existence of religion can be proven for any period earlier than 1000 B.C. He supposes religion to have been an *invention* of some one, and its so general acceptance to have been due to three causes, namely: "the unconscious vanity of its founders, a belief in the happiness which it procures to its believers, and the substantial advantages which society derives from it."

To this theory that religion is in the last analysis a form of selfishness, we may reply that so to regard it, is to set at defiance alike the general testimony of human consciousness and the most manifest facts of history. The religion of millions is directly opposed to their selfishness, which it constantly condemns. Religion has, in fact, been the chief spring of whatever of unselfishness has brightened the history of our race. Nor even were the contrary assertion conceded, would it yet be explained how, even so, religion should have secured such universal acceptance. A man may be selfish in the highest degree, but he is not on that account able to believe in the existence of anything and everything which for selfish reasons he may regard as desirable. Surely there must have been some reason besides human selfishness for the so extensive acceptance of religion.

Many philosophers and theologians have made religion to consist in desire, or *feeling*. So the author of "Natural Religion" defines religion as "a habitual and permanent feeling of admiration"; Mill, as a "craving for an ideal object"; Goethe, as "a feeling of reverence for what is above, around, and what is beneath us." Teichmüller makes religion to consist of feelings of fear, of æsthetic feelings, such as admiration for the beautiful, and of moral feelings.

Among definitions of this class, most important and influential, probably, has been that of Schleiermacher, who says that religion "considered simply in itself, is neither a knowing or a doing, but a determination of the feelings."[1] That which distinguishes the religious feeling from all other feelings is said to be this, that "we are conscious of ourselves as absolutely

---

[1] "Der Christliche Glaube," 5te Ausg., S. 6.

dependent."[1] It should be well understood that Schleiermacher did not by these words intend to exclude either knowledge or action from religion, but only to deny that the essence of religion consisted in either of these. He argues that religion cannot consist in knowing, else the man who knows most would be the most religious;[2] neither in action, else the religiousness of an action would be determined by its own inherent character, as bad or good, as significant or absurd; but actions of every variety, the best and the worst, the most significant, and the most silly and absurd, are recognised by some as religious; whence he infers that the religiousness of any act must be determined, not by its own essential character, but by the feeling of which it is the expression.[3]

It is to be admitted that this well-known definition rightly calls attention to the fact that a feeling of dependence upon an invisible Power beyond man's control, is manifested, in one form or another, in all religions. Even the Buddhist

---

[1] " Der Christliche Glaube," 5te Ausg., S. 5.
[2] Ib. S. 11.   [3] Ib. S. 12.

regards himself as in bondage, not indeed to a person, but to the mysterious power known as *Karma,* which has determined all his thinking, feeling, and acting, his suffering and enjoyment.

Nevertheless, as has often been pointed out, the definition of Schleiermacher is inadequate. It is so because, on the one hand, a feeling is inconceivable, which does not suppose a previous perception or cognition of something, as its occasion; and, on the other hand, this feeling of dependence, which is an element in all religion, universally prompts to action. It is not accurate, therefore, to represent feeling as any more essential to religion than knowledge or action. Nor, again, although all religion expresses a feeling of dependence, is it true that this is the only feeling which is essential to religion. It was Hegel's rather rough criticism of this definition, that if it were true that the sentiment of dependence was the one essential element in religion, then a dog would be the most religious of all creatures; a remark which must be admitted to be not wholly without reason.

Hegel's own definition, however, we must also reject as inadequate, that religion is "perfect freedom." In this we understand him to refer to the fact that in the consciousness of every free moral agent, there is a contrast and a conflict between the actual and the ideal. And whereas man, in his efforts to realise the moral and spiritual ideal, ever feels himself resisted and thwarted by forces without and within him, it is, as he regards it, distinctive of religion that man therein escapes from this bondage, so that his inner impulses are no longer in conflict with his aspirations after moral and spiritual perfection; and in reaching forth unto perfection, he is thus thwarted no longer. The thought has been finely expressed by Principal Caird, who tells us that it is of "*the very essence of religion* that the Infinite has ceased to be merely a far-off vision of spiritual attainment, and ideal of indefinite future perfection, and has become a present reality." [1]

But if the definition of Schleiermacher was at

[1] "Philosophy of Religion," p. 294. Italics not Principal Caird's.

fault in that it centred religion in the feelings, as that of Fichte, in knowledge, so is this faulty in that it centres all in the will. It may be readily granted that religion concerns the will, and that so closely and necessarily, that where there is no willing, there cannot be said to be religion. But we can no more restrict religion to the volitional, than to the emotional or the cognitive faculty.

It has also been justly objected to this definition, and to others essentially like it, that it logically excludes progress in religion, in that it apparently disallows the existence of religion where anything less than this perfect spiritual freedom and inner harmony of the soul with God is found. Nor is the answer which Principal Caird has given to this objection satisfactory. He has said that the religious life is indeed a progressive one; but that the infinite ideal is not realised "only in the way of adding perpetually to the sum of its spiritual attainments," in which case the infinite perfection of the ideal "would be forever unattainable."[1] The infinitude of

[1] "Philosophy of Religion," p. 295.

thought, of love and goodness, is "not that which has in it no element of finitude, but that which is determined by nothing external to itself." To attain the ideal in this sense, he says, "constitutes the very meaning and essence of religion."

For, again explaining himself, he says that religion is "the surrender of the finite will to the infinite, the abnegation of all desire, inclination, and volition, which pertain to me as this private individual self, . . . the absolute identification of my will with the will of God." And this "oneness of mind and will, with the Divine mind and will, is not the future hope and aim of religion, but its very beginning and birth in the soul. To enter on the religious life is to terminate the struggle between my false self and that higher self which is at once mine and infinitely more than mine."[1] But, assuredly, there is much in the world which may be truly called religion, which cannot be so described. Surely, Hindoos and Mohammedans are often deeply and intensely religious; yet, from every side we hear

[1] "Philosophy of Religion," pp. 296, 297.

among them the confession, and most of all from their best men, that the struggle between self-will and God's will is not with them at an end. This is not even true of the Christian. It is, instead, his chief trouble that he has not yet reached the absolute identification of his will with the will of God. Like the Apostle Paul, he is constantly constrained to confess, "I find a law that when I would do good, evil is present with me." We conclude, therefore, that all definitions which, more or less explicitly, make religion to consist in "perfect freedom," err, not merely in that they regard only the volitional part of man's nature, but also in that they make that to be of the essence of religion, which only belongs to the complete ideal of the Christian life ; a goal which the most profoundly religious in all lands and ages have the most earnestly and sadly insisted that they had not yet attained.

Among the most recent important definitions of religion is that which has been given by Professor Max Müller, in the Gifford Lectures for 1888, viz.: "Religion consists in the perception of the infinite under such manifestations as are able to influence the moral character of man."[1] This is a considerable improvement on his earlier definition of religion, as given in his lectures on the Science of Religion, in 1873, and repeated, although with less confidence, in the Hibbert Lectures, in 1878; namely, that "religion is a mental faculty which, independent of, nay, in spite of sense and reason, enables man to apprehend the Infinite, under different names, and under varying disguises."[2] He himself, in these later lectures, justly remarks that in the earlier definition he did not lay sufficient emphasis on the practical side of religion. There is perhaps room in this definition, as not in the former, for the suggestion, at least, of the ideas of law and obligation, as connected with religion. Still the objection holds good against the earlier and the later definition alike, when read in the light of his own explanations, that in them both he uses the word " infinite " in a sense in which it is

[1] "Natural Religion," p. 188.
[2] "Introduction to the Science of Religion," p. 13; "Origin and Growth of Religion," p. 23.

rarely, if ever, employed. He defines it as "all that transcends our senses and our reason."[1] He uses it, therefore, as interchangeable with the words, "the invisible," "the unknown," the "indefinite." One cannot but feel that, as was not unnatural perhaps for a philologist, he has been misled by an etymology. He has apparently reasoned that since the finite is that which is apprehended by the senses as having limits; the in-finite is the not-finite, *i.e.* that which is not apprehended by the senses as having limitations.[2] But surely that is not the sense in which men commonly use this word. In order to perceive this, we only need to apply the word, as used by Professor Max Müller, to many objects which transcend the senses. For example, the human soul transcends the senses. But is it therefore infinite, as men use that term? Professor Max Müller, indeed, apparently limits the application of the word to "the Cause beyond

[1] "Origin and Growth of Religion," p. 27.
[2] Yet he says, quite correctly, that the infinite "cannot be treated merely as a negative concept." — Ib. p. 20.

all causes."[1] But certainly it is no more true of this First Cause than of a multitude of secondary causes, that it transcends the senses. For the immediate causes of a large part of the operations of nature transcend the senses; shall we, therefore, apply the term "infinite" to these? If the definition be correct, why restrict the term to the "Cause beyond all causes"?

Perhaps the definition may seem less unsatisfactory, at the first, to some, because the term "infinite" is so often used as an epithet of the Supreme Being. But in the Professor's vocabulary this term has no such exalted and precise meaning. This is plain from the words which he substitutes for it as equivalents. For instance, in replying to those of his critics who have complained that they were unable to see any difference between the term "infinite," as employed by him in his argument, and the word "indefinite," he says that he "can quite sympathise with them," because he himself can see "none what-

[1] "Natural Religion," p. 124.

ever!"[1] Shall we, then, substitute this latter term, and define religion as "the perception of the indefinite"? and will this be any more satisfactory, although it is added that in religion "the indefinite" is perceived under such aspects as to influence the moral character of man?

Again, Professor Max Müller rightly remarks that the terms used in a definition of religion should be such as to be applicable to all religions; and he is at some pains to show that his definition has this excellence. He says: "I know of no religion that cannot be caught in this wide net."[2] We will admit that this may be true of Buddhism, which is his special illustration; but how about its applicability to the Christianity of the New Testament, or to the inner experience of New Testament Christians? Would it be just to describe the religion of the

---

[1] "Physical Religion," p. 298. He tells us, indeed, that in the Hibbert Lectures he wished to prove "that indefinite and infinite are in reality two names of the same thing"; and that "the Infinite must always remain *to us* the Indefinite."—"Origin and Growth of Religion," p. 36.

[2] "Natural Religion," p. 190.

Apostle Paul as a perception by him of the indefinite, in such a way as to influence his conduct? Will any Christian recognise this as a description of his own case, that in his religious life, his apprehension of the Infinite is nothing more than an apprehension of the indefinite? Such questions answer themselves, and in the answer condemn the definition before us.

Where so many of eminent scholarship and ability have failed, one may well feel diffident in suggesting anything else. But may we venture on something like the following, as a definition of religion in its broadest sense?

Religion essentially consists in man's apprehension of his relation to an invisible Power or powers, able to influence his destiny, to which he is necessarily subject, together with the feelings, desires, and actions, which this apprehension calls forth.

In justification of this definition it is to be observed, first, that it makes religion to be an experience which has to do equally with every part of our nature. Religion does not consist in knowledge merely, nor in feeling merely, nor in desire or willing merely, but in all of these, combined in a necessary and inseparable relation. In the first place, there is in all religion a cognitive element, an apprehension of something supersensual. This apprehension is indeed variously interpreted by different peoples and races, but always there is an apprehension of something. Without this, obviously, a feeling of dependence, for example, could not arise; much less any desire or action of a religious character.

We further define this apprehension to consist in the cognition of a Power or powers. Of the nature of such Power or powers nothing is affirmed, so far as the definition is concerned; it may be real or imaginary, one or many, personal or impersonal. The apprehension, however, becomes religious, if it regard man as dependent in some way on that Power or powers.

The definition is therefore applicable to every form of religion, from the lowest superstition to the highest type of Christianity. It applies, for instance, to fetishism. For that which makes the fetish to the apprehension of the savage that which he imagines it to be, is the belief that, connected with that bit of wood, or bone, or whatever it may be, is an invisible power able to affect his life. The definition applies equally to all pantheistic systems of religion, as, for instance, to Hindooism, whether philosophical or popular. The former recognises a Power behind all that exists, by the activity of which everything is certainly predetermined. It is impersonal, but it is, above all else, a Power; nay, *the* Power. Popular Hindooism worships its many gods, but all are conceived of, as, however diverse in other respects, always powers, able to influence the destiny of man.

And this definition will include even Buddhism. For although orthodox Buddhism recognises no God as determining human affairs, it still regards the life of man as determined; not, indeed, by *Brahma*, or any or all of the gods which it recognises, but by *Karma*. *Karma* means "action"; and what I am has been determined by *Karma;* that is, by the power of the whole eternal series of activities in that chain of existence in which I am a single link. And, as my present, so shall also my future be determined by this same mysterious power, the power of Action. It is true that here the religious idea is reduced to an extreme attenuation. The Power is no longer a god, still less. the One God, personal and almighty; not even a God in the pantheistic Brahmanic sense, impersonal, unconscious. But yet it is admitted that there is a Power, superior to that of the individual man, or of the whole of mankind, which absolutely determines all that concerns us.

In the second place, the definition makes religion also to include an emotional element. Fundamental in every religion is a feeling of dependence on the Power or powers believed to exist. Then out of this feeling arise other feelings, according as man conceives the nature of the object or objects of the religious sentiment. At the one extreme, we find fear, often of a very gross and earthly kind; at the other, reverence, rising at last to an adoring love, like that with which the Christian regards God in Christ, revealed as Love incarnate and dying for man's redemption.

Finally, with the cognitive and the emotional element in every religion are always combined desire and volition, taking effect in various actions. These, naturally, vary according to the mode under which the invisible Power is conceived. Most fundamental is the desire to attain and maintain such a relation to the Power or powers believed in, as shall promote the worshipper's well-being, here and hereafter; and according to the way in which the Power is conceived, will be those determinations of the will by which it is sought to attain a satisfactory relation thereto. Hence there is abundant room in the definition for the most diverse and morally opposite actions, by which religion in different peoples finds expression; whether in the noble devotion to the present and eternal well-being of all men which is the ideal of Christian character; or in the revolting cruelties by which multitudes in other religions have sought to commend themselves to the Power or powers they have worshipped; or, in the absolute asceticism of the ideal Buddhist, who forsakes the world, that he may ever live "alone like a rhinoceros,"[1] without ties, without affection to anything that is.

Religion, then, according to our definition, is a complex experience consisting in the apprehension by man of the existence of an invisible Power or powers, determining his destiny, together with the feelings, desires, and actions to which this apprehension gives rise.

This definition being granted, we are now prepared for the inquiry as to the origin of this experience. And inasmuch as the feelings, desires, and actions, included in the definition, are called forth by the apprehension of the existence of an invisible Power or powers, with which man stands in a necessary relation of dependence, the question as to the origin of religion resolves itself into this: How did man first come to believe in the existence of such a Power or powers, as related thus to himself and to the universe? And this leads us to

---

[1] See "Khaggavisâna Sutta," s. 2, 4, in "Sacred Books of the East," vol. x, part 2, p. 6.

examine some of the more noteworthy of those theories which in our day have been propounded, and have been accepted by many as a satisfactory answer to this question.

LECTURE II.

RELIGION AND NATURAL DESCENT. FETISHISM AND ANIMISM.

BEFORE proceeding to the particular discussion of some of the more popular theories by which it is sought in our day to account for the origin and growth of religion, it is desirable to consider for a little an important postulate which their advocates commonly assume as the basis of their argument. It is usually taken for granted, and often formally asserted by such, that primitive man certainly could not have been superior in intellectual and spiritual capacity to the lowest modern savage races; if, indeed, he was not inferior to the lowest of them. And this postulate itself is rested on another assumption not yet proved, or provable : namely, that man originated in a manner exclusively natural, as the result solely of a long process of development, from one or more pairs of anthropoid apes. If this may now be assumed as ascertained scientific truth, then the above postulate as to the intellectual and spiritual capacity of the first men, appears to be justified; and it becomes highly probable that since the first men could not have been much in advance of their simian parents, religion may have originated in some such way as is supposed in the theories to be hereafter reviewed.

This assumption is so fundamental to these naturalistic theories as to the origin and growth of religion, that it appears indispensable, as preliminary to any detailed criticism, to consider somewhat carefully the question whether this may or may not be rightly taken for granted now as scientific truth, and made the basis of an argument leading to so momentous conclusions.

In opposition to this naturalistic postulate, we venture to affirm that the origin of man by a mere process of natural descent from an inferior order of the animal kingdom, cannot yet be affirmed as established scientific truth. We are, of course, well aware that the contrary is often persistently asserted, and that by men of repute in the scientific world. But it may well make any intelligent layman hesitate to accept a theory so momentous in its consequences on the whole system of scientific and religious truth, when it is observed that the argument which is supposed by many to justify the assertion of the origin of man by merely natural processes, is not accepted as conclusive by authorities who are at least as competent to form a trustworthy judgment as any who affirm this.

The eminent Professor Virchow of the University of Berlin, as president of a recent gathering of the German and Vienna Anthropological Societies, held in Vienna, speaking on this point, used the following words: —

"When we met in Vienna twenty years ago, . . . there was a general expectation that man's descent from the ape or some other animal, would be demonstrated. . . . This, Darwinism has not, up to the present time, succeeded in doing. In vain have the links which should bind man with the ape been sought; not a single one is to be recorded. The so-called "Fore-man," the *Pro-anthropos*, which should represent this link, has never yet been found. No man of real learning professes that he has seen him. . . . Perhaps some one may have seen him in a dream, but when awake he will never be able to say that he has come across him. Even the hope of his future discovery has fallen far into the background; he is now scarcely spoken of; for we live not in a world of imagination or dreams, but in an actual world, and this has shown itself extremely unyielding. . . . At present we only know that among archaic men none have been found that stood nearer the ape than men of to-day. . . . It is clear that among all uncivilised tribes there is not a single one that would stand at all nearer to the ape than to us."[1]

In the presence of such testimony as this, from such an authority, one who moreover by no means stands alone in this position, it

[1] Translated from the *Correspondenz Blatt der deutschen Gesellschaft für Anthropologie*, in the "Journal of the Transactions of the Victoria Institute," vol. xxiv, 1890, pp. 258-260.

should be evident that no one has yet a right to base a theory of the origin and development of religion upon the assumption of the existence of a kind of demi-man in a bygone prehistoric age, when the existence of such a being has never yet been proved. This were to desert that scientific method, to which theologians are so often, by their opponents on the scientific side, earnestly exhorted to adhere.

In the second place, in further criticism of this naturalistic assumption, it is to be remarked that a singular confusion often appears in the argument by which it is supported. It is urged that we are confronted by a large and constantly increasing body of ascertained facts, such as can only be rationally accounted for on the supposition that man has originated through lineal descent from a lower order of the animal kingdom, — a statement which we are not in any wise concerned here to dispute. But those who take for granted the truth of this statement, very commonly at once assume, further, that all evidence which tends to prove, or is thought to demonstrate, such a lineal connection of man with some anthropoid ape, is no less evidence of a *purely natural* evolution.

But this assumption is demonstrably false. For the proposition that man was derived from the lower orders of the animal kingdom through a process of descent, and the proposition that such descent, because one factor, was therefore the only factor in his origination. are far enough from being identical. It is perfectly thinkable that man should be genetically related to other orders of the animal creation, and that, none the less, his appearance should be due to a supernatural interposition of the creative Power. (To prove such/ lineal descent is one thing; to prove that this is the whole and sufficient explanation of man's origin, is quite another matter; and one, we venture to submit, which will be found vastly more difficult.)

Hence, if any feel constrained to concede that the investigations of the past generation have made it highly probable that man has lineally descended from some inferior order of the animal kingdom, this by no means logically forbids us, as some imagine, still to affirm a direct, supernatural, creative interposition of God, as a co-factor with the natural process, and essential to the origination of man. Perhaps one may be allowed, with the deepest reverence, to draw an illustration from the teaching of Holy Scripture, regarding the holy incarnation. The Church in her creeds has universally recognised the fact affirmed in the Gospels, that Jesus Christ was born of Mary, and was thus connected with our race by lineal descent through his mother. But the affirmation of this natural birth, neither in Holy Scripture nor in the faith of the Church, has ever been regarded as exclusive of the affirmation also of the supernatural conception of our blessed Lord in the womb of the Virgin, so that He was no less Son of God than Son of Man. The Christian doctrine of the holy incarnation is thus itself a demonstration that, logically, the natural and supernatural are not, in any event, necessarily exclusive the one of the other. Whether the reality of the Incarnation be granted or not, the fact of the so wide acceptance of the doctrine as representing a historic fact, is proof that, according to the laws of thought, the co-operation of the natural and the supernatural in the production of a certain new order of being, is perfectly conceivable.

Nor is this suggestion of a possible co-operation of a genetic with a creative process in the genesis of man, merely a last resort of despairing theologians, in view of the accumulating evidence of some such lineal connection between man and the lower orders of creation. Alfred Russell Wallace, certainly one of the foremost evolutionists of our time, who shares with Mr. Darwin the origination of the theory of the origin of species by natural selection, in his latest published work, expressly affirms this as a conclusion to which he has been compelled, *on scientific grounds*, by certain indisputable facts. He says: —

"I fully accept Mr. Darwin's conclusion as to the essential identity of man's bodily structure with that of the higher mammalia, and his descent from some form common to man and the anthropoid apes. The evidence of such descent appears to me to be overwhelming and conclusive. . . . But this is only the beginning of Mr. Darwin's work. . . . His whole argument tends to the conclusion that man's entire nature and all his faculties, whether moral, intellectual, or spiritual, have been derived from their rudiments in the lower animals, in the same manner, and by the action of the same general laws, as his physical nature has been derived. *This conclusion appears to me not to be supported by adequate evidence, and to be directly opposed to many well ascertained facts.* . . . To prove *continuity* and the progressive development of the intellectual and moral faculties from animals to man, is not the same as proving that these faculties have been *developed* by natural selection. . . . Because man's *physical* structure has been developed from an animal form by natural selection, it does not necessarily follow that his *mental* nature, even though developed *pari passu* with it, has been developed by the same causes *only.*" [1]

[1] "Darwinism," pp. 461, 463. Italics our own.

In illustration of this, Mr. Wallace then instances the mathematical, the musical, and the artistic, faculties, as facts which compel us to postulate for them some origin wholly distinct from that which may suffice to account for the animal characteristics, whether mental or bodily, of man. He says: "These special faculties we have been discussing, clearly point to the existence in man of something which he has *not* derived from his animal progenitors — something which we may best refer to as being of a spiritual essence or nature. . . . These faculties could not possibly have been developed by means of the same laws which have determined the progressive development of the organic world in general, and also of man's physical organism."[1]

The higher faculties in man, he then argues, "point clearly to an unseen universe — to a world of spirit to which the world of matter is altogether subordinate." And he thus concludes, — while insisting with the utmost confidence on man's derivation from the animal

[1] "Darwinism," pp. 474, 475. [2] Ib. p. 476.

world by a process of descent, as regards all that pertains merely to his animal nature,—that, nevertheless, for the introduction, at successive epochs, into the world, of unconscious, conscious, and, finally, of intellectual and moral, life, as we see it in man, "we can only find an adequate cause in the unseen universe of Spirit."[1]

These words of Mr. Wallace well deserve to be carefully considered. It is quite time that intelligent men should cease to confound things which widely differ, and recognise the immense difference between evidence of descent as *one* factor in the origin of man, and evidence of descent as the *only* factor in the origin of man. And in estimating the value of many fashionable theories as to the origin of religion, it is of the first importance to keep this clear distinction in mind. We cannot allow men—above all, in the name of exact science—to smuggle into the premises of their argument a mistaken assumption of the identity of things that differ; an assumption, which, as appears, according to

[1] "Darwinism," p. 478.

scientific authority perhaps second to none, is not justified, or is even in contradiction to indisputable facts.

The bearing of all this on all the current evolutionary theories of the origin and growth of religion is evident. When Pfleiderer, for instance, tells us that primitive man ("could not have been conscious of his superiority to other animals, nor of his personality, and his spiritual nature"); and that his religion could only have been "a kind of indistinct and chaotic naturism,"[1] he uses language which, however defensible, if man be the result merely of forces resident in organic nature, is without any justification, if such naturalists as Mr. Wallace be right. For if man, although lineally connected with forms of life below him, yet owes his existence to the creative interposition of a Power from the unseen and spiritual world, then there is not the slightest reason for assuming that the first men must have been of such an exceedingly low order as Pfleiderer and others suppose; but rather

[1] See "Encyclopædia Britannica," article, *Religions*, p. 370.

for believing what all archaic remains of men hitherto found distinctly indicate, that in intellectual and moral capacity, the primitive men were fully equal to their descendants of to-day.

Let us not be misunderstood. We are not in the least concerned to maintain that the first men must have been the equals of the modern races in respect of actual attainment. Rational considerations, modern discoveries, and the record in Genesis, all alike require us to deny this. Not only could not the first men build pyramids and hanging gardens, but, according even to the Biblical record, man at first went naked, was then clothed with skins; was ignorant of the art of working in metals, as of other arts. Nevertheless, it does not follow from this deficiency in attainments for which time was necessarily required, that the primitive man must have been such a semi-idiot as the animistic or the fetish theory of the origin of religion supposes. All the evidence as yet before the world, is clearly to the contrary.

Admitting, then, that modern investigation has revealed a multitude of facts which seem to point more or less distinctly to a relation of descent between man and the inferior creatures, we still affirm, without hesitation, that modern science has not thereby advanced a single step toward the proof of a *purely naturalistic* evolution; and that, therefore, all those theories of the origin of religion which assume such a semi-bestial condition as characteristic of the first men, and from this assumption argue as to what was and was not possible to primitive man in religious thought, are essentially unscientific; unscientific, in that they assume that to be proved, which as yet is not established as fact, but still remains in the region of pure hypothesis.

After this brief examination of the presupposition on which the theories to be reviewed in these lectures fundamentally rest, we may now consider them more in detail. We begin with the animistic and the fetish theories, which may conveniently be treated together. It is a familiar fact that many tribes of little or no culture and civilisation, regard with a superstitious reverence and fear, various inanimate objects, such as stones, sticks, shells, etc., in which they suppose a supernatural power to reside. Such objects are called fetishes; and the regard and reverence which is shown to them, "fetishism" or "fetish-worship." This has been supposed by many to represent the most primitive form of religion, still surviving among such peoples.

Tiele, however, very properly classifies fetishism with what he calls "spiritism," under the broader name of "animism"; which last he defines to be the belief in souls or spirits, of which "those upon which man feels himself to be dependent, and before which he stands in awe, acquire the rank of divine beings, and become objects of worship."[1]

So long as these spirits are regarded as disembodied, he calls this form of animism "spiritism." But, he adds, these spirits may also be regarded as "taking up their abode, either

---

[1] "Encyclopaedia Britannica," article, *Religions*, p. 380.

temporarily or permanently, in some material object, whether living or lifeless, it matters not; which object, as supposed to be endowed with a higher power than belongs to it by nature, is then worshipped or employed to protect individuals and communities."[1] Such an object, thus regarded, he defines to be a fetish, and the worship and reverence paid to such objects is fetishism.

This fetishism, by Des Brosses and others, in former times has been supposed to represent the earliest form of religion, out of which all other forms have arisen by a process of natural evolution. Professor Tiele, however, while believing that fetishism exhibits a very early type of religion, does not regard it as absolutely primitive; but with good reason argues that animism, or the worship of spirits, must logically be supposed to have preceded it. Elsewhere he expresses a belief that man in his primitive stage "must have regarded the natural phenomena on which his life and welfare depended, as living beings, endowed with superhuman,

[1] "Outlines of the History of Religion," 4th ed. p. 9.

magical power."[1] According to this animistic theory, therefore, religion originated in a mistake of the primitive men, who ignorantly supposed various natural objects to be alive like themselves, and endowed with superhuman power. But even if we should grant this hypothesis of a primitive animistic naturism, in so far as regards the worship of those objects which, if they have not life, yet in the power of movement have a certain semblance of life, still we should be as far as ever from accounting for the worship of inert objects regarded as fetishes. If one can conceive how ignorant men, seeing objects moving of themselves, might argue with themselves that they must be endowed with an invisible life or spirit, such as they recognised as the cause of their own activities, yet this does not explain an original veneration of such inert, dead objects, as sticks, stones, and shells, which never appear as if endowed with life and power, but the opposite.

For the theory of an original animism as the

[1] See article *Religions* in the "Encyclopaedia Britannica," above cited.

earliest form of religion, Professor Tiele has argued, in substance, as follows: —

" 1. The most recent investigations indicate that the civilisation of the primitive men was of no higher type than that of the present savages; nay, it had not even advanced so far; and in such a civilisation no purer religious beliefs, ideas, and usages are possible, than those which we find among existing communities.

" 2. The civilised religions whose history ascends to the remotest ages, such as the Egyptian, the Akkadian, the Chinese, show still more clearly than later religions the influence of animistic conceptions.

" 3. Almost the whole of the mythology and theology of civilised nations may be traced without arrangement or co-ordination, and in forms that are undeveloped and original, rather than degenerate, in the traditions and ideas of savages.

" 4. Lastly, the numerous traces of animistic worship in higher religions are best explained as the survival and revival of older elements."[1]

[1] "Outline of the History of Religions," pp. 8, 9.

These assertions have not been allowed, however, to go undisputed. To these and other arguments for the origin and subsequent development of all religions from an original worship either of nature-spirits or of fetishes, based on an ignorant misinterpretation of natural phenomena, stand opposed many weighty considerations.

Animism and fetishism alike evidently rest upon an assumption as to the status of the primitive man, which, as we have seen, cannot be scientifically justified.

Again, we cannot safely argue from the case of the modern savage to that of the first men, and infer the beliefs of the former from what we may now see in the latter. The languages of many of the most degraded savages show in a most convincing manner that in them we see, not beings very like the primitive men, but, on the contrary, greatly degenerated types.

The Rev. Mr. Comber, in his valuable "Grammar and Dictionary of the Kongo Language," tells us that in his study of the language he met with "new surprises at every point and turn, as the richness, flexibility, exactness, subtlety of idea and nicety of expression, of the language, revealed themselves."[1] He tells us, further, that "this wealth in idea and form does not specially characterise Kongo, but is possessed by the whole family of Bantu languages to a greater or less extent." He rightly adds that "the widespread possession of these qualities points to their existence in the parent stem, which must itself have been of a high class."

In this he fully agrees with the testimony of the Rev. J. Leighton Wilson, who laboured in another part of the great Bantu language area, among a Mpongwe speaking people. As to the speech of these now fetish-worshipping tribes, he tells us that "this great family of languages, if the Mpongwe dialect may be taken as a specimen, is remarkable for its beauty, elegance. and perfectly philosophical arrangement, as well as for its almost indefinite expansibility."

Similar testimony is given as to the Santâlî,

[1] Op. cit. Preface, p. xxiii.

one of the dialects of the degraded aborigines of India, like the Bantu languages of Africa, only reduced to writing by missionaries. An experienced labourer among that people has told the writer that, in the conjugation of the verb, for example, the Santàlì rivals, if it does not excel, the Greek, in its capacity for discriminating the most delicate and refined distinctions of thought.

But it is needless to multiply illustrations. The facts are now so well known that most competent scholars recognise them, and admit their force. To the great significance of these linguistic phenomena as bearing against the probable truth of the fetish-theory of the genesis of religion, Professor Max Müller has called attention, reminding the reader that the facts are fatal to the assumption of those who, from the present intellectual and spiritual condition of fetish-worshipping tribes, would infer the condition and capacity of primitive men, and by consequence a like low form for their religion. He says:—

"All the stories of tribes without language,

more like the twitterings of birds than the articulate sounds of human beings, belong to the chapter of ethnological fables; and what is more important still, is that many of the so-called savage languages have been shown to possess a most perfect, in many cases a too perfect, that is to say, too artificial, a grammar, while their dictionaries possess a wealth of names any poet might envy. . . . Every language, even that of Papuans and Veddas, is such a masterpiece of abstract thought, that it would baffle the ingenuity of many philosophers to produce anything like it. In several cases the grammar of the so-called savage dialects bears evidence to a far higher state of culture possessed by these people in former times."[1]

Mr. Herbert Spencer refers to similar facts in like terms, warning us that we are not permitted to assume that in modern savage races we see beings very like the primitive men, because "there are reasons for suspecting that men of the lowest types, now known . . . do

[1] "The Origin and Growth of Religion," pp. 72, 73.

E

not exemplify men as they originally were. Probably most of them had ancestors in higher states."[1]

In the presence of such facts as those which have been mentioned, it is obviously of no force to argue that because many savage races now know of no worship except that of fetishes or various nature-spirits, therefore, inasmuch as primitive man cannot have stood higher than these, he could not have had any correct conception of God. If there is evidence that savages are degenerate families of men, then the primitive man may have easily been in religious capacity their superior.

But even if we should not insist on this, and for the sake of the argument grant the assumption that primitive man *could not* have been superior to modern savages; and that hence no religious ideas could have been possible to him other than such as are found among such tribes to-day; still this would not suffice to prove that either fetishism or animism must have been the primitive form of religion.

[1] "Principles of Sociology," vol. i, p. 93.

For, unfortunately for Professor Tiele's argument, it is a fact to which there is abundant unimpeachable testimony, that even among the lowest fetish and demon worshipping tribes, commonly, if not always, we find coexisting with their superstitious religious beliefs and practices, the belief in an invisible personal God, above all spirits and fetishes. The researches of modern travellers, and especially of missionaries, who have lived for years in daily intercourse with such people, have cast in recent years a flood of light upon this subject. Statements such as have been made by Sir John Lubbock and others, to the effect that such and such tribes have no idea of God, have received again and again conclusive refutation, through a careful and critical review of the testimony they adduce, in the light of a fuller knowledge of the facts. The extensive discoveries of the past generation have revealed the existence of no tribe so low as not to have been able to form any conception of God. Instead of this, they have so often reversed previously held opinions to the contrary, that they give us rather reason to believe that when all the facts shall have been carefully investigated, we shall probably not find a single tribe, however addicted to the worship of demons and spirits, which has not, along with this, also the conception of a Supreme Spirit, upon whom all things in heaven and earth depend. The degraded tribes of the west coast of Africa have long with good reason furnished a typical illustration of the characteristics of a fetish-worshipping people. But with regard to these, the missionary, Rev. Dr. J. Leighton Wilson, in his work before quoted, tells us concerning the tribes in Northern and Southern Guinea:—

"The belief in one great Supreme Being who made and upholds all things, is universal. Nor is this idea imperfectly or obscurely developed in their minds. The impression is so deeply engraved upon their mental and moral natures, that any system of atheism strikes them as too absurd and preposterous to require a denial. . . . All the tribes in the country with which the writer has become acquainted, and they are not a few, have a name for God, and many of them have two or more, significant of His character as a Maker, Preserver, and Benefactor."

Of the relation in which this prevailing idea of God stands to the prevailing worship of fetishes, Dr. Wilson gives the following explanation: —

"The prevailing notion seems to be that God, after having made the world and filled it with inhabitants, retired to some remote corner of the universe, and has allowed the affairs of the world to come under the control of evil spirits; and hence the only religious worship which is performed, is directed to these spirits, the object of which is to court their favour, or ward off their displeasure."

Such a phenomenon, then, as fetish or spirit-worship existing alone, and without any accompanying belief in a supreme Spirit, who is above all fetishes and other objects of worship, is yet to be certainly pointed out. Hence the argument for the animistic or the fetish theory, which is based upon the contrary supposition, breaks down, as without any established foundation in fact. And we may rightly insist that if it be thus possible for men so debased in the scale of intelligence as some modern savage tribes, to have the concept of one invisible, spiritual, supreme God; then, even if the primitive man was no higher than they, such a belief may have been possible to him too, and his religion may not after all have originated in the blundering of superstitious ignorance.

Nor is this argument weakened if, as required alike by modern discoveries and the intimations of Holy Scripture, we admit that the first men could not have been called civilised, but were ignorant of the most common arts of life. For it is another mistaken assumption which underlies this argument for a primitive animism or fetishism, as the original type of religion, that the development of religious ideas must always be in exact proportion to the degree of intellectual culture and civilisation which an individual or a race may have attained. The facts prove that this is not true. Indeed, the reverse is so often seen that it would be a more hopeful task to attempt to show that these tend to maintain an inverse ratio to each other. But, to say no more, history shows beyond dispute that there is no constant and necessary relation between the advancement of an individual or a race in intellectual and material civilisation, and the development of religious ideas.

It is one of the most conspicuous phenomena in human life, that very often religious conceptions of a very high order appear among peoples and individuals who have made comparatively little progress in intellectual culture; while, on the other hand, very high attainments in the latter often coexist, as in ancient Greece and Rome,— and, alas, in too many of our modern states,— with something approaching to a paralysis of the religious sense, and avowed or practical atheism. On this point, again, Professor Max Müller has remarked decisively:—

"No one would venture to maintain that religion always keeps pace with general civilisation. . . . We see Abraham, a nomad, fully impressed with the necessity of the Godhead, while Solomon, famous among the kings of the earth, built high places for Chemosh and Molech."[1] Most American Indians are more religious than was the poet Lucretius.

All this receives pertinent illustration among some savage races of to-day, with whom we find no trace of fetish or spirit worship; while on the other hand among many races of far superior natural intellectual endowments, as, e.g., the Hindoos, the worship of various spirits, and of objects which are regarded as veritable fetishes, prevails extensively. As regards fetishism in particular, Mr. Herbert Spencer again has spoken decisively on this point. He says:—

"How untenable is the idea that fetishism comes first among superstitions, will now be manifest. Suppose the facts reversed. Suppose that by Juangs, Andamanese, Fuegians, Australians, Tasmanians, and Bushmen, the worship of inanimate objects was carried to the greatest extent; that among tribes a little

[1] "Origin and Growth of Religion," p. 69.

advanced in intelligence and social state, it was somewhat restricted; that it went on decreasing, as knowledge and civilisation increased; and that in highly developed societies, such as, for example, those of ancient Peru and modern India, it became inconspicuous. Should we not say that the statement (that fetish-worship was the original form of religion) was conclusively proved? Clearly then, as the facts happen to be exactly the opposite, the statement is conclusively disproved."[1]

But to this it is rejoined, as in Professor Tiele's second argument above given, that, nevertheless, the further back we go in the history of mankind, the more of fetishism and animism we discover; from which it is inferred that animism,—if not indeed something still more indefinite,—must have been the earliest form of religion. Convincing proof of this statement we have failed to find; and we even believe that it will be found impossible to produce it. Professor Tiele refers, indeed, to the

[1] "Principles of Sociology," vol. i, pp. 317, 318.

case of the Chinese,[1] but the illustration is unfortunate. The Rev. Dr. Edkins, long resident in China, and intimately familiar with the Chinese language and history, in his "Religions of China," speaking of a reaction among recent Chinese authors against mediæval philosophy, says regarding them:—

"They have returned to an older system, which regarded the personality of God as a fundamental point; and, though it had no very distinct view on the subject of creation, made such statements in regard to the Providence of God, as to show that the early Chinese had conceptions of the Divine Being far in advance of most pagan nations."[2] He adds elsewhere that "the intelligent among the Chinese . . . say that the ancient Chinese were undoubtedly more religious than the moderns."[3]

Moreover, that special ceremonial which is acknowledged to be the most ancient of all forms of worship in China, is precisely that in which the idea of a personal God, the Maker

---

[1] "History of Religion," p. 8. [2] Op. cit. p. 53.
[3] Ib. p. 91.

of heaven and earth, is most distinctly and powerfully suggested. In this solemn act of the worship of Heaven, the Emperor alone acts, as the representative of the nation. Three times in each year, he performs a solemn public service to the Supreme Spirit of Heaven and of the Earth. With this, it is indeed true that ancestor-worship, and thus a worship of departed spirits, also appears, even in the most ancient times; but there is not the slightest evidence that the latter was the origin of the former.

If, leaving China, we turn to India, we find that the facts with regard to the religion of the Hindoos tell powerfully against the theory of the derivation of all religion either from a primeval fetishism or animism. Of both fetish and spirit worship there is much, no doubt, in the India of to-day, even among the Aryan Hindoos. But all agree that this is a late corruption of the Hindoo religion, which only came in long after the entrance of the Aryans into India, and in consequence of association with the fetish and demon worshipping aborigines whom they found there. The earliest hymns of the Vedas, instead of exhibiting a type of religious belief of a more animistic character than that which now prevails, are distinguished by a freedom from such superstitions, and an elevation of religious sentiment, for which we may seek in vain in the religious literature of modern Puranic Hindooism. There is not a single fact to show that the progress of religious thought in India has been upward from an early fetishism or animism to a more enlightened type of faith, but the exact reverse.[1]

But we are reminded that, as just remarked, the more ancient aboriginal tribes whom the Hindoos found in India worshipped, and still worship, various spirits, whose power they dread, and whom they seek to propitiate. But there are well-attested facts which forbid us to suppose, as Professor Tiele's theory would require, that we have here an instance of the survival to modern times of a primitive form of faith. The Santàls, the most numerous and important of these aboriginal tribes, have a tradition, universally accepted by them as true, that in

---

[1] For a fuller exhibition of the facts, see Lecture VII.

the beginning they were not worshippers of demons as now. They say that, very long ago, their first parents were created by the living God; that they at first worshipped and served Him; that they were seduced from their allegiance by an evil spirit, *Marang Buru*, who persuaded them to drink an intoxicating liquor, made from the fruit of a certain tree. In consequence, they came under the power of the Evil Spirit, and hence, from that time until now, have had to worship and serve him and the evil demons subject to him, instead of the one God of their first fathers. That this remarkable tradition, so wonderfully like the Genesis story, can have been derived from this, through direct or indirect communication with Judaism or Christianity, is apparently, in this case, out of the question; for, from an unknown antiquity, the Santâls, in common with other cognate non-Aryan tribes, holding similar traditions, have lived in the mountains and jungles, far off the lines of travel, commerce, and conquest.

There is thus decisive reason for refusing

to regard the fetishism and polydemonism of the aborigines of India as a survival of a primitive cult. These, like many other similar tribes in other parts of the world, furnish in their ancient traditions a weighty argument, not for, but against Professor Tiele's theory of a primitive animism, or that of an original fetish-worship. Instead then of finding a substantial basis for any such theory of the origin of religion in the literature and traditions of various races, the more that these are known and studied, the more do facts appear like the above, which are irreconcilable with its truth. They are such as show, to use the words of Professor Max Müller, that "the history of most religions might be called a corruption of their primitive purity,"[1] and that "fetishism is really the very last stage in the downward course of religion."[2]

Finally, neither the fetish nor the animistic theory of the origin of religion, if assumed as an hypothesis, accounts for those phenomena con-

[1] "The Origin and Growth of Religion," p. 69.
[2] "Natural Religion," p. 158.

nected with religion which most imperatively demand an explanation. It is said that, in the primitive savagery, men could not have had the idea of a personal God, as the Creator and the moral Governor of all, and of their relation to Him, as dependent and responsible beings. But it is certain that they have it now; and in explanation of this, we are told that religion originated, through a process of natural evolution, from a primitive fetishism or animism; which, again, arose, in the first instance, as the result of an ignorant misinterpretation of nature.

But how is it possible that out of such a chaos of crude superstitions as is described by Tiele, Pfleiderer, and others, should have developed the ideas of responsibility, and of sin, and of guilt? Surely, the more deeply that one thinks what is involved in these conceptions, the more insuperable will appear the difficulty of supposing that religion should have had such an origin as animism or fetish-worship.

LECTURE III.

MR. HERBERT SPENCER'S GHOST THEORY OF THE ORIGIN OF RELIGION.

THE theories of an original fetishism, or a "chaotic naturism," or animism, as advocated respectively by Des Brosses, Pfleiderer, Tiele, and others, we have seen to be inadequate to account for many undoubted phenomena connected with religion. In particular, the explanation of the supposed primitive animism, as due to the extreme ignorance of the first men, who mistakenly ascribed life to everything that moved or exhibited power, postulates a supposition as to their condition which to many will seem, on scientific grounds, more difficult of acceptance than the assumed original animism which it is supposed to explain.

Mr. Herbert Spencer has evidently felt this, and, while maintaining that the original form of religion must have been the worship of spirits, accounts for the rise of this spirit-worship by a theory of his own, which he has worked out, in his "Principles of Sociology,"[1] with his accustomed ability and ingenuity. In his "Essays," he states his theory of the origin of religion in these words:[2] "The rudimentary form of religion is the propitiation of dead ancestors, who are supposed to be still existing, and to be capable of working good or evil to their descendants." But it is evident that on this theory it is to be explained how men first came to believe that those of their ancestors who were dead, were still existing. This belief Mr. Spencer has sought to account for after the following manner.

He begins with the conception of things as visible and invisible.[3] The primitive man observed, for instance, that clouds and stars appear and disappear; the same is true of many things. He observed, moreover, that what is invisible, as, for example, the wind, may

[1] Op. cit. vol. i, part 1. The references hereinafter made are to the third London edition, 1885.
[2] "Essays," 4th ed., vol. iii, p. 102.
[3] "Principles of Sociology," vol. i, pp. 105–108.

F

yet have great power. Hence arose, first of all, the concept of a visible and an invisible condition of existence; and, along with this, the recognition of the fact that, in some cases, at least, that which is invisible may have power. And, because the primitive man perceived that *many* things have a visible and an invisible state, he inferred that this might also be true of *every*thing.

Again, the primitive man finds, for instance, a fossil. From this he concludes that one and the self-same substance may be transmuted into another, having entirely different properties. Also, he sees eggs change into chickens, and trees come out of seeds, to which they bear no outward resemblance. He therefore concludes, again, that not only substance, but form, may be transmuted. This will have been confirmed to his mind by the observation that certain insects and reptiles have the power of changing their colour and form, so as to seem very like that in the midst of which they lie.

But primitive men cannot have had any generalised knowledge. Hence there can have been with them nothing to prevent the belief that such transformations were not merely apparent, but real.[1]

Such a belief in real transformations of various objects, as regards substance, or form, or both, having been thus once established, it will have extended itself without resistance to other classes of things. That is, because the primitive man observed that some things apparently become other things, he therefore concluded that anything might become anything, however unlike itself; for — to use Mr. Spencer's own illustration — "the tadpole, with a tail and no limbs, differs from the young frog, with four limbs and no tail, more than a man differs from a hyena; for both of these have four limbs, and both laugh."[2] Hence this ancient savage, at this stage of his evolution, reached the extraordinary conclusion that every object presented to his senses was not only what it seemed to be, but, potentially, was anything else.

Next in order, we are told, the primitive

---

[1] "Principles of Sociology," vol. i, pp. 108–113.
[2] Ib. p. 114.

man will have applied this theory of things to himself. He sees, for example, his own shadow; he " necessarily concludes the shadow to be an actual existence, which belongs to the person casting it."[1] Yet he observes that, in some cases, a shadow is to a certain extent separable from that of which it is the shadow, whence, now beginning to generalise, he infers that "shadows must be conceived of as existences appended to, but capable of separation from, material things."[2] This line of primitive argument was further confirmed by the observation of reflections in water, and by echoes, etc., all of which will have seemed, to the primitive mind, to justify the notion that with every existence of every kind is associated a second existence, visible or invisible.[3]

Again, as the primitive man could not have been able to distinguish real from apparent existence, so neither, according to Mr. Spencer, could he distinguish with any certainty the animate from the inanimate. Seeing that

---

[1] "Principles of Sociology," p. 115.   [2] Ib. p. 116.
[3] Ib. vol. i, pp. 116-119.

many things which usually appear to be inanimate, sometimes act as if they were alive, and vice versa, he will naturally have concluded that all things are at least potentially alive, even shadows and reflections.[1]

In further explication of the evolution of religion, Mr. Spencer instances the phenomena of dreams. He tells us that the primitive man cannot have had the conception of mind, by the aid of which we are able to explain these.[2] What then could he do but suppose that the dream was a *reality*, in the same sense as the experiences of his waking hours; that, while asleep, he actually went where he dreamed that he went, and really did what he dreamed that he did, and so on? And, since he had not yet the conception of a soul within him, by which he might have sought to explain how he — who, as his fellows will have told him, was all the night

---

[1] This confusion of the living and the not-living, however, in Mr. Spencer's opinion, cannot be strictly primary, but was a result of man's first incipient speculation, — of a "germinal error" rising out of experiences which masked the distinction between animate and inanimate. — "Principles of Sociology," p. 131. See also the whole of chap. ix.   [2] Ib. p. 132.

lying in the same place — might also yet have been elsewhere in the spirit, and done or suffered what he dreamed that he did or suffered, — what could the poor untaught savage do but call to his help that idea of the essential dualism of all things, which he had already evolved? Since his observations of dissolving clouds, and waning moon and stars, of shadows and echoes, had brought him to believe that everything has a visible and an invisible state, how natural it must have been for him to infer that he too was a double being, with a visible and an invisible self! and that this second self could become visible at times, and while the visible self was quietly sleeping, could go and do, or suffer or enjoy, all that he dreamed! And — continuing this very primitive reasoning — how natural, again, to conclude that this invisible self must be that same existence, his mysterious double, whom he often sees accompanying him in the form of a shadow, or gazing at him out of the depths of a lake! And how simply this at once explains how it is that, having reached the conception of an indwelling soul in this fashion, many people have spoken of the disembodied souls as "umbræ," "shades"! They must evidently, once, at some stage of their evolution, have conceived of the soul as a shadow.

In illustration of these so grotesque notions, Mr. Spencer gives numerous examples of such beliefs, as, *e.g.*, from the ancient Peruvians and the hill tribes of Burmah, who are said to believe that in sleep the soul really leaves the body and goes whither it will, and so on.

Occasional instances of somnambulism will no doubt have confirmed the primitive man in his beliefs regarding the explanation of dreams. For in such cases the sleeper is sometimes found actually doing those very things which he dreamed that he was doing. Such phenomena, Mr. Spencer thinks, will probably have seemed decisive evidence to primitive men that men do actually go away during their sleep; that they really do in their sleep what they dream of doing, and may on such occasions even sometimes become visible. It is true, as Mr. Spencer admits, that "a careful examination of the facts would show in this case the man's body was absent from its place of rest." But to this trifling difficulty he thinks it quite sufficient to reply that "savages do not carefully examine the facts."[1]

This brings us now to another stage in the evolution of religion.[2] Inasmuch as in dreams the sleeper meets with various people, both living and dead, he will have naturally inferred — if a primitive man — that he really did meet those people. and that, therefore, not only he himself, but other people also have doubles of themselves; and — which is of critical importance in the evolution of religion — that the doubles of *dead* men may and do sometimes appear after death to those who survive them. Hence dawned in the mind of the primitive man the notion of soul as distinct from the body,[3] and of a life after death; and as, perhaps, in his sleep, he scalped or tortured the dead men who,

---

[1] "Principles of Sociology," vol. i, p. 136.

[2] Ib. chap. x.

[3] "Dream experiences . . . are the experiences out of which the conception of a mental self eventually grows." — Ib. p. 141.

when alive, had been his enemies, and had injured him, he inferred that, in that future life, there might be rewards and retributions.[1]

And so it was, Mr. Spencer argues, that man must have reached at last the idea of another and invisible self, separable from the body, which exists after the body dies, and may then appear as a ghost, and in that *post-mortem* state may either administer or receive reward and retribution. And this, he assures us, is the very earliest and most rudimentary idea which man must have had of a God. His words are as follows:—

"We may hold it as settled that the first traceable conception of a supernatural being is the conception of a ghost. This exists where no other idea of the same order exists; and this exists where multitudinous other ideas of the same order exist."[2]

That is, the fact that the belief in a double of a man, which survives death, appears both among savages and among the most highly

---

[1] "Principles of Sociology," chaps. xiv, xv.
[2] Ib. vol. i, p. 281.

civilised races, is, in Mr. Spencer's judgment, of such decisive significance that even of itself alone it is almost enough to prove that the ghost must have been the primitive type of a supernatural being. For, " whatever is common to men's minds in all stages, must be deeper down in thought than whatever is peculiar to men's minds in higher stages; and if the latter product admits of being reached by modification and expansion of the earlier product, the implication is that it has been so reached." [1]

As consequent upon the above evolution, we are then told that it would follow that the men who had known a dead man when alive, would desire to please him now that he was gone, and to propitiate him, if offended. Herein Mr. Spencer sees the origin of all sacrifice, and of ritual of every kind.

Still further, it is plain that, the more powerful a man might have been when he was alive, the more power would his ghost be supposed to have after death. And inasmuch

[1] "Principles of Sociology," p. 281.

as, through the idea which the child has of the greatness and importance of its parents, men would be specially inclined to worship them after death, ancestor-worship would naturally arise as the earliest form of outward religion. And again, among departed ancestors, those would be most honoured or most feared, who had been persons of the most power for good or evil while in this life; whence the common deification of dead heroes, kings, warriors, and such like. And, as the years went by, the conception of these dead men would be expanded and exaggerated, till, at last, from being at first thought of as *very* strong, *very* wise, and so on, they would be thought of as being *all*-powerful, *all*-wise. And, finally, as the outcome of all, we should naturally find — as we, in fact, he says, do find — that men would at last come to worship the supposed *first* ancestor of their own tribe, or of all men, as being the supreme God, the Maker of heaven and earth.[1]

Such, in outline, is the account that Mr.

[1] "Principles of Sociology," chap. xx.

Spencer gives us of the evolution of the idea of God, and of the origin of all religion. A shadow, an echo, a dream, a ghost, a God, the Maker of heaven and earth, and Supreme Ruler and Judge of all mankind! In support of this theory are marshalled a great number of illustrations of every notion to which reference has been made; — illustrations drawn from every quarter of the world, from all races, and all ages of history. Even facts which at first sight might seem to be at variance with his theory, Mr. Spencer presses into the service of his remarkable argument to prove that the idea of a God of all the earth was developed from the observation of a shadow! Thus, in many parts of the world we find fetish-worship, which other philosophers have supposed to be the original form of religion. But fetish-worship Mr. Spencer regards as a secondary development, easily explained on his theory, as simply an aberrant development of ancestor-worship.[1] The spirit, supposed to be resident

---

[1] "Fetish-worship is the worship of a special soul supposed to have taken up its residence in the fetish; which soul, in common

in the fetish, is an ancestral ghost whose special personality, through lapse of time, has been forgotten, and which is believed to have taken up its abode in the fetish. As for nature-worship, in which others have thought they saw the original form of religion, this also he seeks to account for, on his theory, as a development of ancestor-worship. His words are:—

" When it marks the place whence the race came, a mountain is described in tradition as the parent of the race, as is probably the sea, in some cases; and both also give family names: worship of them as ancestors thus arising in two ways. Facts imply that the conception of the dawn as a person, results from the giving of Dawn as a birth-name. . . . The moon is still a source of birth-names among the uncivilised: the implication being that reverence for it, is reverence for a departed person. . . . Lastly, worship of the sun is derived in two ways from ancestor-worship.

with supernatural agents at large, is originally the double of a dead man."—" Principles of Sociology," vol. i, pp. 313, 314.

Here, conquerors, coming from the region of sunrise, and therefore called children of the sun, come to regard the sun as their ancestor; and there, Sun is either a birth-name or a metaphorical name, given because of personal appearance, or because of achievements, or because of exalted position: whence identification with the sun in tradition, and consequent sun-worship." [1]

Such, then, is Mr. Spencer's theory as to the origin of religion, and such the argument, in brief, by which he supports it. Against theory and argument stand the following considerations.

We have to notice, in the first place, that Mr. Spencer tells us at the beginning of his argument that we shall not be able to determine the truth as to the original faith of man on the inductive method. He says that we cannot settle the question as to what were the religious ideas of the primitive man, by merely taking the lowest types of men known to us, and assuming that their ideas, if not primitive,

[1] "Principles of Sociology," pp. 419, 420.

are, at least, very like primitive ideas. For this would be to assume that in these inferior races we had examples of men still in the primitive state; whereas there is not a little evidence to show that many, at least, of these savage tribes — in whom many have supposed that they had before them types of primitive men — are not developments, but degradations from higher forms. His words deserve to be noted: —

"To determine what conceptions are truly primitive would be easy, if we had accounts of truly primitive men. But there are sundry reasons for suspecting that existing men of the lowest types . . . do not exemplify men as they originally were. Probably most of them[1] had ancestors in higher states. . . . It is possible, and, I believe, probable,[2] that retrogression has been as frequent as progression."[3]

Here, then, is indeed an emergency. It is required, in the name of exact science and after

[1] In an earlier edition followed here the words, "if not all of them."
[2] In the earlier edition he wrote, "*highly* probable."
[3] "Principles of Sociology," vol. i, p. 93.

its method, to ascertain and represent the facts as to the origin of religion. Mr. Spencer's evolutionary philosophy compels him to assume that those ideas must have been most vague and rudimentary; that man did not begin his existence as a moral agent with the idea of God, but gradually evolved it, and therewith grew into a moral agent. For if man came into existence exclusively by means of natural processes, in the way of natural descent, as is supposed by Mr. Darwin and Mr. Spencer, then it would appear certain that the original mammal, — Professor Hæckel's hypothetical *Pithecanthropos*, or whatever it was, — which was the immediate ancestor of man as we know him, could not all at once have risen to the idea of a First Cause and Moral Ruler of the universe. Hence, facts are needed which shall show us how this wonderful evolution of religion and of moral agency proceeded. But, unfortunately, such facts regarding primitive man, according to Mr. Spencer, are wanting, and are likely to remain so. The situation, then, at the beginning of the proposed investigation, is embarrassing. On the one hand, is Mr. Spencer's philosophy, which compels him to assume that man must have come up from a condition of mere animality by a purely natural process of development. On the other hand, are stubborn facts which constrain Mr. Spencer candidly to confess that " most of existing savage races have had ancestors in higher states."

Here, truly, is a serious difficulty. On the one hand, is a certain evolutionary theory as to the origin of man and his primitive condition; on the other hand, stand a large number of ascertained facts which appear to be adverse to that theory. Yet the difficulty is not irremovable. By simply calling to our aid an *a priori* hypothesis, it may be made to disappear. Mr. Spencer tells us that, however difficult it may be, we must endeavour to form some conception of what the primitive man must have been, and we shall then be able to form some trustworthy conception of what must have been his primitive *ideas*. This may indeed be difficult; but Mr. Spencer has encouragement for us. He says: —

"The doctrine of evolution will help us to delineate primitive ideas in some of their leading traits. Having inferred, *a priori*, the characters of those ideas, we shall be, as far as possible, prepared to realise them in imagination, and then to discern them as actually existing."[1]

This is certainly candid and clear; whether the proposed method be strictly scientific, is another question. That method is, in a word, as follows: first form the conception of what the primitive man must have been, according to the principles of the Spencerian philosophy, and then seek for facts in nature and history which may be used to confirm the truth of that conception.

This hypothetical primitive man is described by Mr. Spencer in the following language:—

"The primitive man does not distinguish natural from unnatural, possible from impossible, knows nothing of physical law, order, cause, etc.; . . . he lacks fit words for carrying on inquiry, as well as the requisite power of continued thinking. We see that, instead of

[1] "Principles of Sociology," vol. i, p. 97.

being a speculator and maker of explanations, he is at first an almost passive recipient of conclusions forced on him. Further, we find that he is inevitably betrayed into an initial error, and that this originates an erroneous system of thought which elaborates as he advances."[1]

On these postulates as to the condition and character of primitive man, Mr. Spencer bases his argument as to the origin of religion as given above. If ever there was such a being as Mr. Spencer's *a priori* primitive man, then his theory as to the origin of religion might possibly be true; if not, then the theory falls to the ground. But to assume the original existence of such a being, is to beg the whole question at issue. For the point in debate between Mr. Spencer and Christian thinkers, is just this: Did man begin his existence with the idea of God, correct, although undeveloped, or did he only attain this by slow degrees? But since the idea of God involves the idea of a First Cause, Mr. Spencer, in assuming that the first man could not have

[1] "Principles of Sociology," vol. i, p. 13.

had the idea of cause, assumes that he *could* not have had the idea of God, and that hence he did not have it. This, we repeat, assumes in advance the question in debate.

Here we might be content to rest the whole case as regards Mr. Spencer's argument, until some one shall have furnished the proof that ever on earth there existed such a race of idiots as the Spencerian "primitive men." Meanwhile, we have the highest scientific authority for saying that all facts hitherto discovered point the other way.[1] Even Mr. Spencer is not far from admitting this.

To all this it will no doubt be rejoined by many, that Mr. Spencer is justified in assuming the existence of such a being as his hypothetical first man, on the ground that the origin of man by evolution from lower orders of the animal kingdom must now be regarded as accepted scientific fact. But to this we reply that if by the evolution of man is meant that, as regards the *totality* of his nature, and *all* of his faculties, man was the resultant, *solely*, of very gradual

---

[1] See Professor Virchow's recent testimony, cited above, pp. 30, 31.

natural processes, then we deny that it is true that this theory of man's origin can be justly regarded as finally settled scientific truth. By Professor Virchow, it is emphatically declared to be not proved; by Mr. Alfred Russell Wallace, such a theory is declared to be absolutely irreconcilable with indisputable facts regarding man's faculties as compared with those of the inferior animals.[1]

If, on the other hand, by this assertion it is only meant that it is now very generally agreed that man, as regards certain parts of his complex nature, is connected by natural descent with the higher orders of the animal kingdom, the assumption of this as a fact gives no adequate ground for assuming such a primitive man as Mr. Spencer exhibits to us. For if this is all that is intended by the phrase "the evolution of man," then, as remarked before, there is in this nothing which excludes the supposition, that in order to the origination of man, a Power exterior and superior to nature interposed, as Mr. Wallace maintains; in which case

[1] Vid. sup. pp. 35-38.

it is plain that it is by no means certain that the first man must have been a creature of such a low order as Mr. Spencer assumes. If not, certainly, in attainment, yet in endowment and faculty, he may easily have been altogether the equal of the men of to-day; even as is indicated by the earliest crania yet discovered.

All the facts ascertained up to the present day tend to show that man appeared suddenly upon the planet, and then not as a muttering man-monkey, but, in all essential particulars, as really and truly a man as the man of to-day. There is not a particle of evidence that such a creature as this hypothetical man ever existed, except in the dreams of the modern naturalistic evolutionist philosophy.

But, again, in Mr. Spencer's argument it is assumed that there are no innate ideas; that the notions of cause, responsibility, etc., and all other so-called intuitive ideas, are the product of experience. Even if true, this would not be self-evident; a multitude of the world's deepest thinkers have believed that there was abundant evidence that these ideas are innate and intuitive. If such as these have been right, then it is certain that there was something in the constitution of the primitive man, no less than in our own, in virtue of which he naturally and necessarily conceived of things in the relation of cause and effect. To build up a theory to account for the origin of religion, and leave out of consideration the idea of *cause*, as of necessity involved, explicitly or implicitly, in all thinking, is not permissible. For no one is able to adduce a single instance of a people so low that they have not exhibited the causal judgment in full operation. It constantly appears that, however crude and erroneous notions any people may have as to the nature of God, they are constrained to believe in His existence, in part, at least, because compelled to believe that every event must have an adequate cause. There are absolutely no facts to sustain Mr. Spencer's allegation that the primitive man knew nothing of cause.

It is another remarkable and most suggestive fact that, in Mr. Spencer's elaboration of his theory as to the origin of religion, he has practically ignored the phenomena exhibited in man's consciousness of sin. One might almost imagine that he had never heard that any race of men believed in such a reality as sin. The index of his "Sociology" is exceedingly full and satisfactory, filling fourteen finely printed pages, but we have not found the word "sin" or any of its equivalents in any of those pages! But this is not surprising; for he has constructed his whole theory of the origin of religion, without any serious reference to this omnipresent and very solemn fact of man's consciousness of sin; although it is an element which appears even in the lowest types of religion!

This omission is specially noticeable in his account of the origin of sacrifices. It is one of the most notorious facts connected with the customs of men concerning sacrifice, that, as a general rule, these stand more or less distinctly connected with ideas of placation and propitiation. It is indeed true that Mr. Spencer, in this connection, freely uses the words "propitiate" and "propitiation"; but it is plain that he does not use these words in their ordinary sense. For example, he illustrates the nature of "propitiation" by "the wish to do that which a lately deceased parent is known to have desired." We submit that in such desire there is nothing of the sentiment which we connect with the word "propitiation": that the word invariably connotes the idea of displeasure or wrath in the person to be propitiated, which by the propitiation it is sought to remove. Sacrificial rites, if not universally, yet very extensively, rest upon the assumption, more or less distinctly made, that, in man's relation to the supernatural Power, or powers, to whom the sacrifice is offered, there is something wrong, something, at least, which needs improvement. The failure to account for this and other common phenomena connected with man's sense of sin, is one of the most remarkable defects in Mr. Spencer's argument. To attempt to construct a theory of the origin of religion, and omit to grapple earnestly with the facts regarding sin, as he has done, is very much as if a man should construct a theory of the heavens with no special reference to the law of gravitation. Such attempts have indeed been made in the region of physical science, but they have led to no valuable result, and are interesting chiefly as evidence of the ingenuity of the men who made them.

It is another grave defect in Mr. Spencer's theory that it fails to account for the whole content of the idea of God. It does not show us how the conception of a self-existent First Cause, — which, according to Mr. Spencer, man did not have at first, — could possibly be developed out of the idea of a shadow or a ghost. He tells us, indeed, that "no other causes for (unexpected) changes are known or can be conceived" by the primitive man; and therefore he reasoned that "the souls of the dead must be the causes."[1] But this assertion needs to be proved; and until proved, what right has Mr. Spencer to say that the primitive man did not

---

[1] "Principles of Sociology," vol. i, p. 217. This seems curiously inconsistent with the statement above cited (p. 82) that the primitive man could not have had the idea of cause.

and could not conceive of any cause of the phenomena of the universe, of which these souls were parts, other than the souls themselves?

Again the conception of a God, as we have it, also includes the conception of a Power to which we are responsible and which we have displeased, and which therefore requires to be propitiated. How could these ideas, again, of responsibility, sin, and propitiation, be developed out of one's relations to a ghost or a shadow? Mr. Spencer does not show us. He teaches, indeed, that propitiatory rites had their origin in funeral ceremonies, designed to secure the favour of dead ancestors, "conceived chiefly as the causers of evils";[1] but he does not seem to see that this leaves unexplained the very thing which most needed explanation; namely, why it should ever have occurred to men that the spirit of a dead friend would be likely to injure them. Rather should we infer that they would naturally have thought of a

[1] "Principles of Sociology," vol. i, p. 277. See the whole of chap. xix.

departed father or mother, for instance, as still cherishing the former parental love.

Mr. Spencer has indeed made a very extensive collation of facts which he claims as substantiating his theory as to the origin of religion. We cannot here review them in detail, but only remark that, however many of these facts may be consistent with his theory, they are no less easily accounted for in other ways; while, besides those which he adduces, there are many other facts, to some of which we shall have occasion to advert, which are utterly irreconcilable with his theory.

Once again, if Mr. Spencer is right in assuming that the worship of a personal God is everywhere and always a development from a prior ancestor-worship, then it is plain that the lower the moral and intellectual state of any people, the less and less distinct we ought to find the idea of God; while, on the other hand, the worship of ancestors should be by so much the more prominent. So also it should follow, if Mr. Spencer's theory were true, that, everywhere, the more ancient a people, — in other words, the nearer we approach to the days of Mr. Spencer's primitive man, — the more we should see of ancestor-worship, and the less of the recognition and worship of God.

It is indeed true that history presents many instances in which men after their death have come to be regarded as gods. Such was the case with the Buddha, with Rām and Krishna, in India, and with many others in other lands. But such instances of the deification of dead men do not occur under such uniform conditions as we should expect to find, if ancestor-worship were in reality the original form of all worship and all religion.

It is not true, in the first place, that as a rule it is the most degraded tribes who are most given to the worship of ancestors. Neither is it true that among such the idea of God is always dim in proportion to the development of ancestor-worship. Mr. Spencer indeed gives abundant evidence that tribes of a low rank are often addicted to ancestor-worship. But this fact, of itself, proves nothing to the purpose. Such instances can be just as readily accounted for on the Christian belief, that there has been in such cases a degradation from an earlier conception of God. Mr. Spencer needed to show that the worship of ancestors has been the universal historical antecedent of the worship of God. This he has not proved, and — we venture to add — it cannot be proved. The reasoning by which Mr. Spencer attempts to prove it, is sufficiently remarkable to deserve notice. It may be put, for the sake of clearness, in the form of a syllogism, thus: —

"The feeling out of which worship grows up, must be a feeling which is common to all men; the dread of ghosts is a feeling common to all men, while the fear of God is not. Therefore the dread of ghosts must be the feeling out of which the worship of God must have grown." Which reminds one of the formula of erroneous logic: "All A is B; but all C is B: therefore, all C is A."[1]

Again, instead of its being true that there are tribes who worship ghosts or the spirits of their ancestors, but have not yet reached

[1] "Principles of Sociology," vol. i, p. 281.

the idea of God, as remarked in the previous lecture, it cannot be shown that anywhere there is a tribe so degraded as not to have, in some form or other, the idea of a God, quite distinct from the ordinary objects of their worship. Dr. Livingstone assures us that "there is no need of beginning to tell the most degraded of the people of South Africa of the existence of God or of a future state, both these facts being universally admitted." The Rev. J. Leighton Wilson, long a missionary on the west coast of Africa, gives the same testimony as to the degraded natives of that part of Africa.

Even if, however, we should admit the existence, here and there, of tribes who have no conception of God, as a certified fact, it would prove nothing as to the truth of Mr. Spencer's theory as to the origin of religion. It would, no doubt, be consistent with it, if true; but it would be equally consistent with the supposition that man began his history with a knowledge of God, which such tribes have lost. We must not forget that Mr. Spencer himself concedes that "most savage tribes have had ancestors in higher states."

Mr. Spencer quotes, indeed, asserted instances of tribes who have not even a name for God; as, *e.g.*, Indians found in 1776 by Father Serrain about San Francisco Bay, and certain South American tribes; and refers also to the well-known assertions of Sir John Lubbock on this point, though with a hesitating endorsement.[1]

For such hesitation there is indeed good reason. For no one who has had any experience in endeavouring to communicate on the subject of religion with a strange people, and that in an unfamiliar language, will be disposed to accept such statements as true, except after the most searching investigation, of which, in this case, we have no evidence. Misapprehensions of fact in regard to this matter have been so very numerous, as to call for the utmost care in the weighing of testimony. Professor Flint has criticised a large number of such statements concerning various tribes, and has shown conclusively that the testimony on which these rest was either erroneous, or,

[1] "Principles of Sociology," vol. i, p. 281.

in other cases, has been misunderstood.¹ It is not by such a smattering of a savage tongue as a sea-captain may casually pick up, or a passing traveller in a foreign land may gain, that one becomes able to gain accurate information as to the religious opinions of a savage people. The testimony of such men, therefore, as Captain Cook, who is quoted as authority by Mr. Spencer as to the religious beliefs of the Fuegians, is by no means to be accepted without hesitation.² In like manner, Sir John Lubbock quotes a certain Mr. Jukes as authority for the assertion that the natives of the Dalrymple Islands are atheists, but it appears that this Mr. Jukes — an honest man, no doubt — was only one day on the island; nor is his testimony more than negative, to the effect that in that one day he was not able to discover among the natives any trace of a belief in a God.

Among civilised peoples, the facts tell powerfully against Mr. Spencer's theory. In no land

---

[1] See "Antitheistic Theories," Notes xxvi–xxxi, pp. 259–281.
[2] "Principles of Sociology," vol. i, p. 316.

is the worship of ancestors more extensively practised than in China, and we have the advantage of being able to trace the religious history of China with confidence to a very remote period. But, in the earliest period of which authentic Chinese records tell us, the worship of Heaven was co-existing with that of ancestors. Dr. Edkins tells us that, along with this ancestor-worship, the Chinese have had the tradition of one Supreme Ruler "from the earliest period of their history."[1] 'There is no evidence that the idea of God was any less distinct, or, on the other hand, that the worship of ancestors was any more prominent, in the earliest ages of Chinese history than at present. Whether it be true or not that the ancient Chinese worship of Heaven was in reality the worship of the one, true, invisible, God — a point on which the authorities differ — there is no evidence that this worship of Heaven was an evolution from a primitive worship of ancestors.

Of a similar character in their bearing on

[1] "Religions of China," p. 95.

the argument of Mr. Spencer, are the facts as regards the religious history of India. The deification and worship of dead men is indeed very common in modern India; but it is the fact, which Mr. Spencer ought to know as well as any one, that, the further one goes back in the history of the religions of India, the less there is of this ghost and ancestor-worship, and the clearer and more frequent is the recognition of one God, the Father of all and the Giver of all good. And when we go back to the days most remote in antiquity, before the Vedas were written, when the whole Indo-Germanic race were living, as yet undivided, on the plains of Iran, we find that at that time there was no such state of things as Mr. Spencer's theory would require. There was not more of the worship of ghosts and ancestors then than in Vedic and post-Vedic days; but, as Professor Fairbairn has shown, more clearly recognised then than ever since, was the idea of one Supreme Being, the Father of all and the Lord of the conscience, *Dyauspitar*, the "Heaven-father," — a "Person, whose 'thou' stood over against the 'I'" of the worshipper, and that "no ghost of a dead ancestor seen in feverish dreams!"[1]

Yet another pertinent illustration of our argument is afforded by the history of ancient Egypt. The primitive religion of Egypt presents to Mr. Spencer's, as to every false theory of the history of religion, a most decisive and fatal test. The wonderful progress made of late years in the discovery and decipherment of the literary remains of that most ancient people, enables us to speak with assured confidence. And what is the testimony of those venerable authorities? Was ancestor-worship first, and was the idea of God a late development? Assuredly not! In contradiction to the assertions of Professor Tiele, and regardless of the exigencies of Mr. Spencer's theory of religious evolution, M. Renouf, in the Hibbert Lectures for 1879, has shown most conclusively that the earliest form of Egyptian religion was *monotheistic.* Detailed proof of this statement may be reserved for a subsequent lecture.[2] It

---

[1] "Studies in the Philosophy of Religion," p. 43, Amer. ed.
[2] Lecture VII.

will be sufficient here to refer in a general way to the testimony of this eminent Egyptologist, that, although in Egyptian literature there are frequent references to various gods, such as Horus, Osiris, Ra, and Set, yet a "Power" (*Nutar*), "without any individual name or mythological characteristic, is constantly referred to in the singular number, as the Power from whom all other powers proceed."[1]

Was then this "*Nutar*," the God of primitive Egypt, perhaps only a deified ancestor, the first king of Egypt, or the first man, as Mr. Spencer's theory would have it? For this there is not a vestige of evidence. M. Renouf's answer to this question is most unambiguous. He affirms that the Power thus named is no ghost of the first king of Egypt, or of the first ancestor of the race, but "unquestionably the true and only God, who is not far from any one of us."

Neither, according to this same distinguished scholar, can this ghost-theory of religion

[1] For references for these and the following citations from Renouf, see Lecture VII.

account even for the subordinate gods, which, along with the true and living God, the Egyptians came to worship. M. Renouf is very explicit on this matter. He says that these subordinate gods of ancient Egypt " were not the ghosts of ancestors or other dead men, or representatives of abstract principles, as ancient and modern philosophers have supposed, . . . but the powers of nature." The extreme antiquity to which we are able to trace back the history of religion in Egypt, through the witness of contemporaneous documents, makes it in a special manner a test case for all theories on this subject. If in Egypt we find no trace of ancestor-worship as the antecedent of the worship of one God, then we are not likely to find it elsewhere. The consentient testimony of all reputable Egyptologists is such as to make it clear that the facts as regards the early religious history of the Egyptians cannot be comprehended under Mr. Spencer's theory.

We have been greatly surprised that Mr. Spencer should also argue for his theory from the original meaning of the words which are used in many languages to denote "God." His words are: "Even the words applied in more advanced societies to different orders of supernatural beings, indicate by their original community of meaning, that this has been the course of genesis. The fact cited above, that among the Tannese the word for 'a god' means literally 'a dead man,' is typical of facts everywhere found."

In reply to this we have to ask for evidence that such facts are "everywhere found." It is not given, as it should have been, in his argument. In the meantime, we venture to question this broad assertion, and submit the following facts to the contrary.

Among the Chinese, the word *shin*, used for "God," means originally, according to Chinese scholars, "breath," and then, "spirit." Among the ancient Hindoos, as also among the moderns in South India, the word *deva*, for "God," is derived from the Sanskrit *div*, "to shine," and has nothing to do with a dead man. Neither have other words used to denote the Divine Being, in North and South

India, any reference to the spirits of the departed. The etymology of *Brahma* is uncertain, but has been thought by high authority to denote God as the worshipped one (from *vṛih*, "to increase"?). The word *Ísh* (*Íshwar*) means "lord." *Deus*, as every scholar knows, is connected with the Sanskrit *divas*, from *div*, as above. The yet older name *dyaus*, preserved for us in the syllable *Ju*, of *Jupiter*, etymologically means "heaven," and has never been used in any language with reference to the dead. Connected with this Sanskrit *dyaus*, also, are the Greek *Zeus*, the Old German *Ziu*, the Anglo-Saxon *Tiw*, the Gothic *Tius*, and the Scandinavian *Tyr*. The etymology of the Greek θεός is yet uncertain; but, among all the derivations which have been suggested, there is not one which embodies any allusion to dead ancestors. The term *Ahura-mazda*, by which God was known among the ancient Zoroastrians, is compounded of *ahura* (for the Sanskrit *asura*, "living one," "the eternal") and *mazda* (from *maz*, "great," and *dao*, "knowing"), and is thus, literally, "the omniscient Eternal." No suggestion here, evidently, of some dead ancestor.

Among the Hebrews and other Semitic peoples we have many names for God, but not one, so far as we are aware, which affords any semblance of support for Mr. Spencer's astonishing statement. *Yahveh* (Jehovah), like the old Egyptian *Nuk pu nuk*, probably denotes the Supreme Being, as Mr. Spencer should know, with reference to his self-existence. The Hebrew *El* (Assyrian *Ilu*), etc., as also the ancient Egyptian *Nutar*, by etymology denote God simply as the Mighty One. The Hebrew *Elohim, Eloah* (Arabic *Allah*), from a root meaning "to tremble," represents the Supreme Being as the object of awe and worship. Such terms as *Baal, Adoni,* "Lord," "my Lord," and *Molech,* "monarch," etc., no doubt are applicable enough to some great ancestor or earthly monarch, but there is not the slightest evidence that they originally had this reference.

But such facts as these, if known to Mr. Spencer, do not seem to have troubled him. He even represents the Old Testament as supporting his theory, quoting Isa. viii. 19: "And when they shall say unto you, consult the ghost-seers and the wizards that chirp and that mutter; should not a people consult their gods, even the dead, in behalf of the living?"[1] So also he refers to the case of the Witch of Endor (1 Sam. xxviii. 17), as seeing "gods" coming out of the earth, among whom appears the dead prophet Samuel.[2]

But what have these passages to do with the proof of his position? They imply, no doubt, that the people addressed were in the habit of worshipping, or, rather, consulting, the dead; but that does not prove that this worship of the spirits of dead men *preceded* the worship of God, so that the idea of God is to be *derived* from the conception of a ghost.

But the case of the Jews, notwithstanding these words from Isaiah, gives Mr. Spencer no little trouble. How to reconcile the facts con-

---

[1] So Mr. Spencer translates! but see the revised version, as also Delitzsch, and many other expositors of the first rank.
[2] "Principles of Sociology," vol. i. pp. 298, 299.

cerning their history and worship with his theory, is the problem, and he does not seem to have found it an easy one. He deals with it in the following manner.

In the first place, he admits that the earliest Hebrew "legends" are silent on the subject of ancestor or ghost-worship. But, he rejoins, "the silence of their legends is but a negative fact, which may be as misleading as negative facts often are." Very truly said! Silence as to such worship would not of necessity prove that it did not originally exist. But, unfortunately for Mr. Spencer's argument, the Hebrew writings are not silent as to the worship of primitive men, but have spoken most distinctly about it. They emphatically and unanimously testify that the Hebrews, and, indeed, the human race, began, not with ghost-worship, but with the worship of a living and personal God. But this testimony is passed over by Mr. Spencer in silence. Possibly, however, he may have had this in mind when he next remarks that the sacred books of a religion "may give very untrue ideas concerning the actual beliefs of its professors,"[1] and suggests that this may be the case with the writings of the old Hebrews. In support of his theory of an original Hebrew ancestor-worship, however, he ventures upon citing Deut. xxvi. 14, wherein the sacrificer is required to say that he has not given of his first-fruits "for the dead." From this passage he concludes that ancestor-worship had then developed "as far as nomadic habits allowed, before it was repressed by a higher worship." But granting that the words imply the worship of the spirits of the departed at the time when the book was written — which no one would think of denying — what bearing has this on his argument? For the conclusion to be established is not that ancestor-worship is *ancient*, but that it was *primitive*. The words prove the former, but have no bearing on the latter.

So far, then, in review of Mr. Spencer's theory of the origin and the evolution of religion. We can readily recognise the ingenuity of his reasoning, and the extensive

---

[1] "Principles of Sociology," p. 292.

research which this part of his Sociology exhibits; but none the less are we persuaded that, as an hypothesis to account for the phenomena of religion, his theory, no less than that of a primitive animism or fetishism, must be regarded as inadequate and unsatisfying.

LECTURE IV.

PROFESSOR MAX MÜLLER'S THEORY OF THE ORIGIN OF RELIGION.

VERY different from the theories hitherto reviewed, is that which in various successive publications has been elaborated by Professor Max Müller. Unlike many others who have written on the subject, he is professedly, not an unbeliever, but a believer in the Christian religion. Regarding Christianity, — or, to speak more accurately, Christianity as he understands it, — he never speaks but in the highest terms. He declares it to be his conviction that "there is no religion in the whole world, which in simplicity, in purity of purpose, in charity and true humanity, comes near to that religion which Christ taught to his disciples."[1] This attitude of his toward the religion of Christ as understood by him, no doubt inclines many

[1] "Natural Religion," p. 570.

to receive his theory as to the origin and growth of religion the more readily, as thus presumably in harmony with the teachings of the Holy Scriptures and the fundamentals of Christian faith.

In judging the value and significance of his estimate of Christianity, and the presumable relation of his theory to the Christian religion, it is, however, necessary to bear in mind that his words in praise of the religion of Christ appear only to have reference to the ethical teachings of our Lord. For, in his "Physical Religion,"[1] he explicitly refuses credence to everything which, in those same Gospels which are the only authority as to Christ's moral teachings, He is said to have claimed and taught regarding His own superhuman personality. The accounts which are given by Matthew and Luke of the miraculous conception and birth of our Lord, he expressly classifies with the absurd legends concerning the childhood of Jesus which appear in the Apocryphal Gospels; from which, he tells us,—nothing troubled by

[1] Published in London, 1891.

the absence of all evidence for the truth of the assertion,—these stories have "found their way, we know not through what channels, into two of our Synoptical Gospels!"[1] These accounts of the supernatural origin of our Lord are, therefore, in his opinion, "fabulous stories," "imaginary representations"[2] of no more historical value than the tales of the wonderful birth of the Buddha in the later Buddhistic books, which serve him as an illustration.

Denying thus the truth of that claim for making which, as all extant accounts agree, Jesus of Nazareth was crucified, he thus finds himself quite at liberty to reject everything else in His teaching, as recorded in the Gospels, which, if accepted as true, would be irreconcilable with his own theory as to the origin and development of religion. He thus consistently denies the claim of Christianity, as expounded by its Founder, to be a supernatural revelation and the true religion, in any exclusive sense. The distinction between natural and revealed

---

[1] "Physical Religion," p. 356. [2] Ib. pp. 356, 357.

religion he refuses to admit. While differing radically with Mr. Spencer and Professor Tiele as to the manner of the origin and development of religion, he is quite at one with them in regarding it as exclusively natural, and in denying that man began, or could have begun, his existence on earth, with the knowledge of God as one and personal. "The idea of θεός, 'God,'" he tells us, "was evolved from the idea of θεοί, 'gods'"; [1] it is "the result of an unbroken historical evolution, . . . but not of a sudden revelation," [2] and while the road from nature certainly leads godward, it is only through the gate of polytheism that men have attained to the final belief in one supreme and only God.[3]

In arguing this opinion, he appeals continually to history as preserved in language, but sets aside without hesitation the teachings of those Jewish Scriptures which Christ recognised as of inerrant authority, as unworthy of credence in what they teach as to the origin and development of religion. If Christ and his

[1] "Physical Religion," p. 117.   [2] Ib. p. 140.   [3] Ib. p. 142.

apostles attributed to them any such authority regarding the early history of our race, this only proves that they were mistaken.

In view of the assured confidence with which he sets aside the testimony of the early Old Testament records, as merely an agglomeration of ancient oral traditions and legends, without much historical value, it is truly somewhat surprising to find him, in the Gifford Lectures for 1890, more than two years after the famous tablets discovered at Tel el Amarna had been deciphered by Professor Sayce, his learned colleague in the University of Oxford, yet saying that "to suppose that portions of the Old Testament existed in the form of books in the time of Moses, would run counter to all history";[1] that David's letter to Joab about Uriah (2 Sam. xi. 15) "seems the first authentic specimen of epistolary writing";[2] and that no books were written till "nearly a thousand years after Moses."[3] For, on the high authority of Professor Sayce, we are able to affirm as a matter of certain knowledge, that 150 years

[1] "Physical Religion," p. 219.   [2] Ib. p. 388.   [3] Ib. p. 216.

before the time of Moses, a constant correspondence was going on between Egypt, Palestine, and Babylon, of which the original autographs are in our possession. Moreover, in the light of these facts, Professor Sayce suggests that the existence even of libraries in the land of Canaan at that very early date, is quite possibly intimated by the familiar name of the Canaanitish city of Kirjath Sepher, literally, "City of the Book."[1]

When we thus find facts which bear so decisively on the trustworthiness of the Old Testament records passed by in silence, and statements made, or suppositions advanced, which they conclusively disprove, it is evident that no one should attribute too great impor-

---

[1] See "Transactions of the Victoria Institute," vol. xxiv. pp. 12-27, "Annual Address by the Rev. Professor Sayce." Over against these surprising assertions of Professor Max Müller we may set the following words of Professor Sayce: "Little historical credence can be placed, it has been urged, in the earlier records of the Hebrew people, because they could not have been committed to writing, until a period when the history of the past had become traditional and mythical. But this assumption can be no longer maintained. Long before the Exodus, Canaan had its libraries and its scribes, its schools and literary men."

tance to the professor's estimate of the historic value of those ancient Scriptures which represent a belief as to the beginning of religion so completely contradictory of that which he has elaborated. And it is only right that, in estimating the worth of his reasonings, and the value of his laudations of the Christian religion, one should keep in mind the lecturer's mental attitude toward all supernaturalism in religion, as indicated by such facts as the above.

Notwithstanding, then, the many words of praise for that which he regards as Christianity, Professor Max Müller, no less than the writers hitherto reviewed, rejects the teaching of the Christian Scriptures as to the origin and development of religion, for a theory of his own. He tells us that, instead of man having known, from the first, one personal God as his Father in heaven, "religious thought began with the naming of a large number of clearly marked and differentiated objects, such as the Sky, the Dawn, the Thunder, the Lightning, the Storm, Mountains, and Trees; and that the concept of superhuman beings arose afterward, as a concept common to all, when divested of their characteristic differences."[1] Thus, according to this theory, no less than those previously criticised, the representations of the Book of Genesis concerning the origin of religion, — endorsed, it must never be forgotten, by our Lord Jesus Christ, — are the exact reverse of the truth. Man did not begin with a knowledge, even very rudimentary and imperfect, of his Father in heaven, but with no knowledge of Him whatever. And the history of religion has not been a decline from primeval simplicity and purity, but a steady advance, on the whole, from that which was lower to that which was higher; from naming to nature-worship; from that, through polytheism and henotheism, to monotheism, the recognition of the one God, the Creator and Ruler of heaven and earth.

It was the object of the Hibbert Lectures in 1878, on "The Origin and Growth of Religion," to show, in illustration of this theory, how it was that, in India, at least, man gradually rose, from the mere perceptions of the

[1] "Natural Religion," p. 130.

senses, through what is called "henotheism," and then polytheism, to the recognition of the unity of God. In those Lectures, Professor Max Müller defined religion as a "mental faculty or disposition which enables man to apprehend the Infinite."[1] This definition, as remarked in Lecture I, he has since modified, and, in the Gifford Lectures for 1890, religion is defined as "the perception of the infinite under such manifestations as are able to influence the moral character of man."[2] The "infinite" is defined as comprehending "all that transcends our senses and our reason."[3] And yet he constantly insists that all knowledge, and therefore the knowledge of the infinite, comes through the senses; and thus he makes the validity of his whole argument to rest upon the truth of sensationalism.

After all that has been said, however, the question will still force itself upon us: How is it possible that the idea of the infinite, of infi-

---

[1] "Origin and Growth of Religion," pp. 22, 23.
[2] "Natural Religion." p. 188.
[3] "Origin and Growth of Religion," p. 27; cf. pp. 34, 35.

nite space, for example, could be gained through sense perception? Professor Max Müller's answer to this question we have in such words as the following: "With every finite perception there is a concomitant sentiment, or, if that word should seem too strong, a concomitant sentiment or presentiment, of the infinite." These words he explains as meaning that "from the very first act of touch, or hearing, or sight, we are brought in contact, not only with a visible, but also, at the same time, with an invisible universe."[1] Or, again: "The reason why we cannot conceive an absolute limit is because we never perceive an absolute limit."[2] Hence arises the notion, *e.g.*, of infinite space, or of infinite time. And, in the perception of the infinite thus gained through the senses, he assures us that "we have the root of the whole historical development of human faith."[3] In detail, the theory is then worked out in the following manner.

---

[1] "Origin and Growth of Religion," p. 46.
[2] "Natural Religion," pp. 122, 123.
[3] "Origin and Growth of Religion," p. 47.

Having received an impression of the infinite in their very first sense-perceptions, men began then to look for the infinite in various objects, such as mountains, rivers, trees, the overarching heaven, etc., and, slowly rising higher and higher, generalising the various conceptions gained, they at last began to call that unseen Infinite, Maker, Preserver, GOD!

The history of early religious thought as given in the Veda, and the Vedic language, is then used for the confirmation of this theory. The various objects of sense-perception are classified, for this purpose, as "tangible," "semi-tangible," and "intangible."[1] Under the first head are placed "objects complete in themselves, which we can touch and handle all around, which we can smell, and taste, and hear, as, *e.g.*, stones, bones, shells, flowers, berries, and logs of wood." To the second class, the "semi-tangible," belong such objects as can be apprehended by the senses, but not completely; such as trees, mountains, rivers. Other objects of sense, again, cannot be touched,

[1] "Origin and Growth of Religion," p. 179. *et seq.*

although they can be seen. Such are the sky, the sun, the moon, and the stars. These are called the "intangible"; "in all these percepts the infinite preponderates over the finite, and the mind of man is driven . . . to admit something beyond the finite."[1] In such objects as these, we are told, are found "the germs of most of the great gods of the ancient world"; while the second class, the semi-tangible, has furnished the demi-gods of men, and the first and lowest connects itself with fetish-worship.[2]

Besides this revelation of the infinite in nature, the infinite is disclosed also "in man, looked upon as an object, and lastly, in man, looked upon as a subject."[3] And this threefold source of the idea of the infinite, is made the basis of a distinction between "physical," "anthropological," and "psychological" religion.[4]

This analysis is then illustrated by the history of the development of religion in India.

[1] "Origin and Growth of Religion," pp. 185, 186; "Natural Religion," p. 153.   [2] Ib. p. 154.
[3] Ib. p. 155.   [4] Ib. p. 164.

Professor Max Müller regards it as certain that in the primitive Vedic age, the Indian Aryans did not have the idea of God as we have it. "The concept and name of deity was passing through the first stages of its evolution."[1] The evolution proceeded after the following manner.

"The ancient Aryans first faced the invisible, the unknown, or the infinite, in trees, mountains, and rivers; in the dawn and the sun; in the fire, the storm-wind, and the thunder; they ascribed to all of them a self, a substance, a divine support, or whatever else we like to call it: — in so doing they always felt the presence of something which they could not see, behind what they could see; of something supernatural behind the natural, of something super-finite, or infinite. The names which they gave, the *nomina*, may have been wrong; but the search after the *numina* was legitimate. That search led the ancient Aryans as far as it has led most among ourselves, viz., to the recognition of a Father which is in heaven.

[1] "Natural Religion." p. 203.

Nay. . . . it led them farther still : . . . they learnt, and we all of us have to learn it, that we must take out of that word 'father' one predicate after another, all in fact that is conceivable in it, if we wish to apply it still to God."[1]

And still we are not to understand the professor as teaching that the earliest faith of the Indian Aryans was polytheism. Yet neither was it monotheism, but what he calls "henotheism." The exposition of this term may best be given again in his own words. Man in India began with "a belief and worship of those single objects, whether semi-tangible or intangible, in which man first suspected the presence of the invisible and the infinite, each of which . . . was raised into something more than finite, more than natural, more than conceivable; and thus grew to be an *Asura*, or a living thing; a *Deva* or a bright being; an *Amartya*, that is, not a mortal, and at last an immortal and eternal being, — in fact, a God, endowed with the highest qualities which the

[1] "Origin and Growth of Religion," pp. 228, 229.

human intellect could conceive at the various stages of its own growth."[1] This was henotheism, a "belief in single supreme beings."[2]

The rationale of this process, according to Professor Max Müller, is revealed by the scientific examination of the origin of language. "The most of Aryan words expressed originally our own acts."[3] Most primitive acts "were accompanied by almost involuntary utterances."[4] Man, first using such radical sounds, predicated acts of himself,[5] and then, through the necessity of the case, named all other objects, animate and inanimate, by applying to them these roots expressive of action, which he had used first of himself. "All that had to be expressed had to be changed into actors." "The fire was called *Agni*, 'the moving'; the Dawn, *Ushas*, 'the shining,'" etc., etc. Thus the personification of the powers and phenomena of nature was a necessity arising out of the nature of language; and so language generated the myth, and the myth, religion. If the wind was named

---

[1] "Origin and Growth of Religion," p. 266. [2] Ib. p. 384.
[3] "Natural Religion," p. 386. [4] Ib. p. 387. [5] Ib. p. 388.

Mârut, "the striker," this supposed an unseen power as the agent. And so with all those words which designated the ancient Vedic gods.

This theory of the origin and the order of the development of religion, he attempts to prove by the case of the sun; showing us how "we can follow in the Vedic hymns, step by step, the development which changes the sun from a mere luminary into a creator, preserver, ruler, and rewarder of the world — in fact, into a divine or supreme being." And yet, as is clearly shown, all the divine attributes which are ascribed to the sun, are in like manner ascribed, to the sky, then to fire, and to other objects of worship.[1] And yet this was not, strictly speaking, polytheism; for each of these, for the time being, was regarded and addressed as if it were the sole divinity. And this is what he has named "henotheism."

We may well sum up these statements of Professor Max Müller's by giving his own résumé of his argument in the Hibbert Lectures.

"Our senses, while they supply us with

[1] "Origin and Growth of Religion," pp. 270, 271.

a knowledge of finite things, are constantly brought in contact with what is not finite, or, at least, not finite yet. . . . Their chief work is in fact to elaborate the finite out of the infinite. . . . *From this permanent contact of the senses with the infinite* sprang the impulse to religion, the first suspicion of something beyond what the senses could apprehend, beyond what reason and language could comprehend. Here was the deepest foundation of all religion, and the explanation of that which before everything, before fetishism, and figurism, and animism and anthropomorphism, needs explanation; why man should not have been satisfied with a knowledge of sensuous objects; why the ideas should have ever entered his mind, that there is or can be anything in the world besides what he can touch or hear, or see, call it powers, or spirits, or gods. . . . After the idea had once laid hold of man, that there was something beyond the finite, the Hindoo looked for it everywhere in nature, trying to grasp and to name it; at first among semi-tangible, and then among intangible, and at last among invisible objects. . . . A new world thus grew up, peopled by semi-tangible, intangible, and invisible objects, all manifesting certain activities, such as could be compared with the activities of human beings, and named with names that belonged to those human activities. Of these various names, some became general epithets, and the word '*deva*,' *e.g.*, among them. . . . Other ideas which are truly religious, . . . were, like all abstract ideas, . . . derived from sensuous impressions, even the ideas of law, virtue, infinitude, and immortality. . . . Lastly, by a perfectly natural and intelligible process, a belief in single supreme beings, or *devas*,— Henotheism — tended to become a belief in one God, presiding over the others, no longer supreme gods, Polytheism; or a belief in one God, excluding the very possibility of other gods — *Monotheism*. Still further, . . . all the old *devas* or gods were found out to be but names; but that discovery, though in some cases it led to atheism and some kind of Buddhism, led in others to a new start and the belief in one Being, which is the Self of everything, which is not only beyond and beneath all finite things, as apprehended by the senses, but also beneath and beyond our own finite Ego, the Self of all selves."[1] This last form of belief Professor Max Müller does not name, but the intelligent will recognise it as pantheism.

Fully recognising the learning and ability with which this theory of the origin and development of religion is elaborated by its accomplished author, we must yet regard it as utterly inadequate and unsatisfactory.

In the first place, the whole discussion is vitiated by the sense which is given to the word "infinite," as used in his definition of religion. The term is defined as comprehending "all that transcends our senses and reason," and is repeatedly interchanged with the words "invisible" and "indefinite."

But as this definition has already been criticised at length,[2] we may pass on to indicate another and still more serious objection to the

[1] "Origin and Growth of Religion," pp. 381-384.
[2] Vid. sup. pp. 16-21.

theory under consideration. It is fundamentally based on a false theory of knowledge. Professor Max Müller constantly insists that all knowledge whatsoever, whether religious or any other, in the last analysis, is derived from the sense-perceptions, and comes through the senses only. Of any intuitive perception, intellectual or moral, whether of cause, or of the infinite, or of the distinction of right and wrong, he will hear nothing. Still less will he allow the possibility of any primeval revelation, even though it were given through the senses. Everything which any religion may contain, came in the first instance through the senses, and in a purely natural way. This is affirmed in his writings again and again. Thus we are told in the Hibbert Lectures: —

"All knowledge, in order to be knowledge, must pass through two gates and two gates only, the gate of the senses, and the gate of reason. Religious knowledge also, whether true or false, must have passed through these two gates. At these two gates, therefore, we take our stand. Whatever claims to have entered in at any other gate, whether that gate be called primeval revelation, or religious instinct, must be rejected as contraband of thought. And whatever claims to have entered by the gate of reason, without having first passed through the gate of the senses, must equally be rejected as without sufficient warrant, or ordered at least to go back to the first gate, in order there to produce its credentials."[1] "We know not what the infinite is, but we know that it is, and we know it because we actually feel it, and are brought in contact with it."[2]

It is impossible, in the limits assigned to these lectures, to discuss the whole question of sensationalism in philosophy, but we may call attention to certain considerations which especially bear on the relation of sensationalism to this argument on the origin and growth of religion.

If the word "infinite" be taken in the sense in which men commonly use it, as denoting that which is absolutely illimitable, then it is certain that this idea can never have come to us through the senses. There is more in the concept than sense-perception can possibly furnish. How could the senses assure us of the infinity of space or duration, of which we neither have nor can have any experience?

But this is not all. For the affirmation of the mind is not merely that there *is* an infinite, but that there *must* be an infinite. Professor Max Müller indeed thinks that this too can be explained through sense-perception. He tells us: "The reason why we cannot conceive an absolute limit is because we never perceive an absolute limit."[1] But this is to *condition* the idea of infinity by man's power of perception; whereas the concept, as it lies in the mind, is always that of an absolutely unconditioned truth. Moreover, the affirmation of the infinite, *e.g.*, in space, involves a declaration regarding the future, no less than regarding the present. But how can sense-perception give any man a certitude as to what must be in all the future? It is true that sense-experience gives us a beyond, an immense beyond, or an

[1] "Natural Religion," pp. 122, 123.

indefinite beyond, of space, but certainly not an infinite beyond, which, moreover, must exist forever.

The utter inadequacy of the theory to account for the phenomena of religion is all the more apparent, when we direct our attention from the intellectual "must" to the "must" of moral law. If even the idea of intellectual necessity cannot have come into the mind through the senses, still less, if possible, can that moral obligation which is revealed as an eternal necessity in all the great religions. Professor Max Müller, indeed, apparently thinks this to be sufficiently explained by a reference to our observation by the senses, of the order of the physical universe.[1] But the explanation is inadequate to account for the facts. Even if we should grant — what would be hard to prove — that it was the perception of the physical order of nature which first awakened the idea of a moral order, we should still be as far as ever from accounting for the most essential fact of all, that man apprehends the moral

[1] "Origin and Growth of Religion," p. 251.

order as *necessary*, and conformity to it as of eternal *obligation*. For that no one ever thinks of the order of the *kosmos* as necessary, the common belief in miracles sufficiently attests. But how the idea of that which is necessary, can be evolved from the perception of that which is *not* necessary, the professor omits to show us.

But even if we were to assume the correctness of the definition of the infinite which Professor Max Müller gives us, as " that which transcends the senses," it is still not easy to see how it can be true that " our senses give us the first impressions of infinite things."[1] To most, these two propositions will appear to be mutually exclusive. If either is true, then how can the other be true?

The only apparent escape from this dilemma is by the supposition that when it is said that our first impressions of the infinite are derived from the senses, it is only meant that certain sense-perceptions are the *occasion* of bringing the idea of the infinite into consciousness. But

[1] " Origin and Growth of Religion," p. 38.

if this is what is intended, then it is implied that the idea of the infinite is logically antecedent to the sense-perceptions which call it out into consciousness; and sensationalism is not the whole of philosophy, much less the foundation of religion.

No less irreconcilable with sensationalism is the representation which we find in "Physical Religion," where we are told that the worship of natural objects "owes its origin to the category of causality."[1] But if we grant this, sensationalism fails to explain it. For the causal judgment is not that every phenomenon has had, or has, or even will have, but that it *must* have, an adequate cause. But the question often asked, never has been, and never can be, answered: How can this conception of the *necessity* of causation, be derived from our sense-perceptions?

Even such considerations as these should be sufficient to show the inadequacy of the theory before us to explain the origin of religion; for, on the truth of sensationalism, the theory is

[1] Op. cit. p. 8.

based. Of any apprehension of God by the conscience, prior to and apart from the visible perception of His presence and power in nature, Professor Max Müller will hear nothing. He tells us, that he does not blame any one who may "decline to discuss the problem of the origin of religion with those who assume . . . a religious faculty which distinguishes man from the animal."[2] Everything in religion is traced back to man's sense-perceptions; everything, from the most degraded type of fetish-worship to the Sermon on the Mount, and the Lord's Prayer!

But still greater is the difficulty of evolving from these perceptions of the infinite, or the indefinite, or the beyond, not merely the idea of causation, but also that of a personal God, as First Cause, and moral Ruler of the Universe. Grant that in the perception of an "intangible object," as, *e.g.*, a storm or the sky, men do get the impression of a power or a vastness indefinitely beyond what we can measure and comprehend; what is the reason that men in

---

[1] "Origin and Growth of Religion," p. 128.

all ages have such a tendency to predicate the power or the immensity, — not of the storm, or the sky, but of an unseen God, distinct from storm and sky, who makes the clouds his chariot, and rides on the wings of the wind? Here is a break in the continuity of the supposed development. Even beasts appear sometimes to have vague impressions of an unknown or indefinite beyond that which they see or hear, even as the professor supposes of his ideal primitive man. What else can it be than this, which makes a horse, for example, start and tremble at an unfamiliar sight or sound? But if in such a sense-perception is contained in an elementary way the idea of a personal God, and, as Professor Max Müller tells us, man has no religious faculty different from any possessed by a brute, why, then, should not the horse have ever attained through sense-perception some dim idea of an invisible God? How can we avoid the inference that into the concept derived from the senses man puts something else, which the senses could not have furnished?

According to Professor Max Müller, polytheism was preceded by a form of religion which he calls henotheism; in which, although in name many different gods were worshipped, yet each was regarded by the worshipper, for the time being, as the one only God. The phenomenon is explained by a reference to the necessities of thought as expressed in language. Because, *e.g.*, the Storm-wind presented itself to the senses as that which beats and pounds, therefore it was called *Marut*, "the beater," "the striker"; hence it was necessarily conceived of as a personal being, and so came to be regarded as a god, — nay, under the overwhelming impression of its power, as, for the time being, *the only* God. But this does not explain why these powers of nature should have been regarded as personal; still less, why each or any one of them should have been regarded, even for the time, as the one only mighty God, and the moral Ruler of the Universe. The fact that they were so regarded and addressed, implies that the worshipper already had the conception of power as connected with personality, and the idea of responsibility, and, in particular, of a Deity behind phenomena, from some other source. The truth is, that this peculiar form of religion which is called henotheism is far more naturally and easily explained as the first step in the declension from a primitive faith in one invisible God, the Author and Ruler of Nature, toward the fully developed polytheism which immediately followed. Perceiving God to be manifested in various forms in material nature, men, in the first instance, addressed the worship which was His sole due, to the powers of nature, not as separate from Him, but as manifestations of the God who was One. But from this, it was only a step further in thought to separate these wholly from God, and conceive of the Fire, the Dawn, the Sun, the Wind, each as separate objects of worship.

Closely related to this is another difficulty, namely, concerning the evolution, on this theory, of the ideas of responsibility, and of sin and guilt. For instance, admitting that the ancient Hindoos and other nations received their first impressions of God from the observation of the objects and powers of nature, why should they have proceeded to *identify* the Power revealed in *nature* with the Power revealed in *conscience;* and then regarded themselves as under moral obligation to the Being whose power was revealed in the hurricane? Especially, why should men have universally conceived of themselves as in a relation of disharmony with this Power? Whence, in a word, on this theory, could have come the universal sense of sin and guilt? To refer to the fact that the powers of nature often appear unfriendly to man, is an inadequate explanation, for often, on the contrary, they appear kindly and helpful; while the sense of sin and disharmony with the unseen Being is practically continuous and universal; and is most deeply felt by the purest and the noblest natures. So, in this theory, we see again illustrated that same obliviousness to the profound significance of man's consciousness of sin and guilt, which is so characteristic of modern naturalistic theories of the origin and growth of religion.

But it is time that we turn our attention to the professor's historical argument. He asserts that the genesis and order of the development which he maintains, is historically evidenced by the course of religious thought in India; namely, that the Hindoos began with the worship of what he calls semi-tangible objects, mountains, rivers, etc.; and then gradually rose, through the worship of intangible objects, such as the sun, the moon, the sky, etc., through polytheism, to the worship and recognition of one sole and only God. But the facts which he adduces fail to prove his theory as to the origin and development of religion.

First, because even if we should grant that there was no trace of the recognition and worship of one personal God in the Rig Veda, this would prove nothing as to the absolute beginning of religion. No one pretends that the Vedas give the absolute beginning of religion, even among the ancient Aryans. Even though the earliest form of worship which we find in Hindoo literature is henotheism, or nature-worship, this does not prove that religion began with henotheism, or nature-worship. Why may not this have been a degraded form of religion, which had succeeded to an earlier and purer creed? For that the nature-worship which we find in the earliest Vedic hymns, 1000–1500 B.C., has come down from primitive times, is asserted by no one.

Much is made indeed of the history of the word *deva*, finally applied to God. We are told that the word first meant simply "bright"; then was applied to a whole *class* of objects of worship as "bright ones"; and hence came to mean "a god," as one of many bright ones, regarded as objects of worship; and, finally, came to denote the one supreme God. Hence it is argued that the idea of "God" must have arisen subsequent to the idea of "gods." But the argument is inadequate to establish the conclusion. First, because we have not in this word a record of primitive thought, but of a comparatively late period in religious development. Again, as a matter of fact, we find the idea of a supreme

God existing among ancient races, long before the history of this word *deva* begins.

All that is said with regard to the history of this word loses its force as argument, so soon as we thus recall to mind that it takes us back nowhere near the beginning of religion. To assume that men must have thought of the "bright ones," or "the strong ones," as many, before they could have reached the concept of one Being, to whom brightness or strength could be imputed in the highest degree, is to assume what cannot be proved until we can somewhere find some historical record of the absolute beginning of religious thought, not merely among the Hindoos or the Aryans, but in the whole human race. The history of India, or even of the whole Aryan family of languages, does not take us within sight of this. Indeed, we could not make stronger statements on this point than we find in Professor Max Müller's own writings. Although he asserts, that "in the ancient religion of India" we can "watch the development of religion, though in one stream only, from its very beginning to its very end,"[1] yet, again and again elsewhere, even in the same course of lectures, he himself, in so many words, contradicts this unguarded statement.

Thus, *e.g.*, he says: "There are vast distances beyond the hymns of the Veda, and many things even in the earliest hymns become intelligible only if we look upon them, not as just arising, but as having passed already through many a metamorphosis."[2] So, again, we read: "No doubt between the first daybreak of human thought and the first hymns of praise (in the Veda) there may be — nay, there must be — a gap that can only be measured by generations, by hundreds, aye, by thousands of years."[3] And, yet again, in "Physical Religion" he tells us that in the Vedas much is "secondary, nay, tertiary, and altogether modern, in one sense of the word."[4]

This is all true; and the same may be said of that word *deva*, which is made to carry so much weight in the argument. Even

---

[1] "Origin and Growth of Religion," p. 34.   [2] Ib. p. 85.
[3] Ib. p. 231.   [4] Op. cit. p. 15.

the earliest period to which we can trace it back in the cognate languages, is still also " altogether modern, in one sense of the word." How then can any argument be based upon it, unless one can prove that in this instance the primitive sense of the term had persisted for ages without man having yet been able to clamber up by its aid to the definite conception of one personal God?

In view then of the professor's own more accurate statements, it seems that we cannot, in the ancient religions of India, certainly " trace the development of religious thought from its very beginning to its very end." But if not, then what proof have we from the history of the Hindoo, or even of Aryan religion, that man began his religious life with the adoration of the infinite as revealed through his senses in nature?

In the second place, and apart from this, Professor Max Müller has failed to show that the *order* of religious development in India was such as his theory requires. It was essential to his argument to have demonstrated that the most ancient hymns of the Veda are those which are addressed to semi-tangible objects, such as the soma juice, mountains, rivers, and trees; and to intangible objects, like the sky, the sun, the storm; and that the hymns addressed to one God and Father of all, are the most modern. But this order of succession he has not even tried to establish. It was nothing to the point merely to cite, as he does, from the Vedas, hymns to the mountains, the sun, the heaven, the supreme God, as objects of worship; except he also should prove that the chronological order of these was as his theory required. Singularly enough, this he has not attempted; perhaps it was an impossible task; but the demonstration was none the less essential to his argument.

Not only so, but he candidly admits facts which show that the order required by his theory was not the actual order of history. The worship of the sun, an intangible object, he tells us, preceded that of the class of semi-tangible objects. This looks like a religious degeneration descending to less and less worthy symbols of the Deity as objects of worship. So he tells us that the oldest deity of which we have any trace in the Vedic religion, "one of the oldest, indeed, of the whole Aryan race," was *Dyaus*, which is commonly said to mean "sky," but which he thinks would be better defined as "the bright one," "the shining one," with special reference to the luminous heaven.[1] This deity is often addressed as *Dyauspitar* (Lat. Ju-piter), lit., "Heaven-father." A less worthy symbolism did not precede, but followed, the days when *Dyaus* was God.

So there are hymns in the Rig Veda which express the recognition of and worship of one sole and personal God. According to the theory before us, these should be the latest of all of the hymns. But this is not proved, and there is no reason to suppose that Professor Max Müller believes it to be true.

The fact is, that in the Rig Veda we find side by side with the grossest nature-worship a lofty theism which sometimes reminds us of the Psalms of David. That the former preceded the

---

[1] "Origin and Growth of Religion," p. 282.

latter in the belief of the people, there is not the slightest proof. Most admirable are the words of the professor with regard to the succession of thought in the Vedas; of which he says: —

"By the side of much that sounds recent, there is much that sounds ancient and primitive. And here we ought, I think, to learn a lesson from archæology, and not seek to lay down from the beginning a succession of sharply divided periods of thought. . . . There are in the Veda thoughts as rude and crude as any paleolothic weapons; but by the side of them we find thoughts with all the sharpness of iron and all the brilliancy of bronze. Are we to say that the bright and brilliant thoughts must be more modern than the rudely chipped flints that lie by their side?"[1]

Finally, it is to be remarked as a very singular defect in Professor Max Müller's writings on this subject, that he apparently confounds monotheism with pantheism. It is, indeed, quite true that now and then he uses expressions which — might we but take them by them-

[1] "Origin and Growth of Religion," pp. 239, 240.

selves — would be naturally understood as implying the theistic view of the nature of God. Thus, in one instance, he even says that the idea of one personal God is "the highest form . . . which man feels inclined to give to the infinite":[1] while once and again he speaks of God as our Father in heaven, in words which must find an echo in every truly Christian heart. But, unfortunately, such words do not stand alone, but are interchanged with others, and are qualified and explained in such a way that it becomes very difficult to believe that the writer uses the terms employed in the sense in which Christians commonly understand them.

A striking example of this is found in the passage in which he tells us that " the ancients learnt, and we all have to learn it, that we must take out of that word 'father' one predicate after another, — all, in fact, that is conceivable in it, — if we wish to apply it still to God." It is true that, taken by themselves, such expressions might be interpreted as inti-

[1] "Origin and Growth of Religion," p. 303.

mating such a conception of the nature of the Divine Being as was held and argued by Christian men like Dean Mansell and Sir William Hamilton; a conception which, however, — we do well to remember, — was afterward logically developed into complete agnosticism by Mr. Herbert Spencer.

With Professor Max Müller, however, it seems clear that, if we allow him to interpret himself, these expressions must be understood in a pantheistic sense. Certain it is, that when he speaks so often of the Deity as the "true Self of the world" and "the Self of all Selfs,"[1] he is using forms of speech essentially identical with those which one may hear any day from the Brahmans of to-day on the banks of the Ganges. That our understanding of his words is shared by learned and cultivated Hindoos, is apparently evidenced by the fact that his Hibbert Lectures on the Origin of Religion have been so highly appreciated by the pantheistic Hindoos, that they have been translated by scholarly natives of India into two

---

[1] "Origin and Growth of Religion," p. 384 *et passim.*

or three of the chief vernaculars of that country.

But, surely, when the Hindoo speaks of God as one, he means something very different from that which the Christian theist means, when using the same expression. Monotheism and pantheism are not identical, but denote mutually exclusive beliefs. Christian theism no doubt regards God as μόνος, yet not, like Hindooism and pantheism everywhere, as τὸ μόνον, but ὁ μόνος; not as the Only because the *All*, the only real existence, but as the only true and living God, immanent indeed in all, but far transcending all, in his own eternal personality.

LECTURE V.

THE TRUE GENESIS OF RELIGION.

IF religion did not originate with fetish or spirit-worship, through a mistaken apprehension of all nature as living, nor with the worship of ancestors, nor with the apprehension, through sense-perception, of the infinite, as defined by Professor Max Müller, how then are we to explain its origin?

We reply that in the origin of religion, we have to recognise two factors, the one *subjective*, the other *objective*. The subjective factor we find in the nature of man. We affirm that in virtue of the very constitution of his spiritual nature, man necessarily believes in the existence of a Power or powers, superior to himself, to which he stands in necessary relation, and by which his destiny is determined.

One can hardly express this better than by

saying that man is naturally endowed with a religious faculty. It is not intended, indeed, to distinguish this sharply from the reason, the affections, or the will, as these are distinguished from one another; but simply to affirm that in the normal exercise of all these powers, man is naturally, and almost inevitably, constrained to regard himself as in necessary relation to an unseen Power or powers, superior to himself, and conditioning alike his past, his present, and his future.

That this belief is due, not to education, or tradition, or any other accidental cause, but to the constitution of man's nature, is demonstrated by the fact that religion, in the sense in which we have defined it, is universal. That religion is universal is declared with emphasis by unbiassed specialists like Quatrefages, who has said that "we nowhere find either a great human race, or even a division, however unimportant, of that race, professing atheism."[1] He affirms that two beliefs are practically universal: first, "a belief in beings superior to

[1] "The Human Species," 3d ed. p. 483.

man," and therefore "capable of exercising a good or evil influence on his destiny"; and, second, a "conviction that the existence of man is not limited to the present life, but that there remains for him a future beyond the grave."[1] But where these beliefs are found, there we have religion; religion, then, is universal.

It is doubtless true that religion appears under widely different external manifestations. It may be very elementary, almost devoid of rite or ceremony, or it may be connected with an elaborate symbolic ritual. Man may recognise God as one, or he may believe in gods many; or stranger still, he may, as in the original religion taught by the Buddha, decline to affirm the mysterious Power which determines all. to be in any sense a God; and represent it rather as impersonal and non-substantial, the power of *Karma,* "action." But whatever form the conception of the Supreme Power may take, whether it be regarded as a personal and almighty Being,

[1] "The Human Species," 3d ed. p. 484.

as by the Christian, the Jew, and the Mohammedan; or as the spirit or fetish, worshipped by the savage; or as the nameless "*Adrishta*" or "Unseen" of the Hindoo, or the still more mysterious and incomprehensible *Karma* of the Buddhist; in every case alike, it must be confessed that everywhere and always, man has a religion. This is so manifest, that the denial of the fact, once not uncommon, in our day, after more careful and extensive research, is much more rarely heard. It is commonly admitted that religion is a universal phenomenon, and that exceptions — if any exist — must be regarded as abnormal.[1]

We have, then, to inquire why this should be so; and how it is that religious conceptions and feelings arise thus universally in the mind and heart of man.

The deepest reason of this is to be found in man himself. In the first place, man cannot

---

[1] Of many illustrations which might be given, we may note the emphatic words of Professor Tiele: "The statement that there are nations or tribes which possess no religion, rests either on inaccurate observation, or on a confusion of ideas." — "Outlines of a History of Religion," p. 6.

help recognising that he is a dependent being; dependent, not merely upon other human beings, as his parents, friends, and rulers, but, in common with all of these, dependent upon a Power which is above all men; a Power which man cannot control, and which can effectually dispose of all that concerns him, whether for prosperity or adversity, weal or woe.

Nor have men generally been able to content themselves with regarding this power as merely that of material nature, upon the operations of which their physical well-being depends. It is the fact, whatever the reason may be, that even when natural objects have been worshipped, they have been regarded by the worshipper as something more than merely material objects; as the symbols or the manifestations of an invisible Power or powers. And if we ask why men so often, as in all animistic and polytheistic religions, should have assumed, behind the wind, the storm, the lightning, and other natural phenomena, a living Power, the answer can only be found in the nature of man.

Logically, prior to the consciousness of the

Non-Ego is that of the Ego. But every man who is conscious of self is conscious of that self as possessed of power. Hence, inasmuch as men know in consciousness that the reason for all the movements of the body is found in an invisible power, the conscious self, which has its fullest manifestation in free volition, they are irresistibly constrained to postulate an analogous invisible power, as also the ultimate cause of all activities of material nature. In this, the so-called nature-religions are not wrong, but right. And so it comes to pass that, naturally, the most cultivated and most debased peoples alike regard themselves as in a relation of dependence to an invisible Power or powers. And while we may not, with Schleiermacher, make the whole of religion to consist in this sense of dependence, we shall rightly regard this as one very important factor, on the subjective side, in the genesis of religion.

But man is constrained to believe in the existence of a supernatural Power, not only by his sense of dependence, but by the necessary laws of thought. For undeniably all that is presented to our perceptions is presented as conditioned and contingent. And the more that man advances in his knowledge of the universe, the more clear it becomes that this is a universal fact. But this being so, man is logically compelled to believe in the existence of somewhat which is not conditioned, but conditioning, itself ever remaining unconditioned; a power, not contingent, but necessary, apart from which neither man nor the world could have existence. For of the conditioned, the conditioning is the necessary correlate, such that the former cannot be thought without the thought of the latter; even as the affirmation of a circle carries with it by necessary implication the affirmation of a centre of that circle. In this way, again, man is compelled, no less as a reasoning being than as a dependent being, to believe in an invisible Power, to which he and all the universe stand in necessary relation, and on which the welfare of all depends. And in this fact we have further evidence that the origin of religion is to be found in the very nature of man.

But this is not yet all. Man universally is possessed of a faculty which we call conscience. In view of now well-ascertained facts, the assertion of some earlier writers, like Sir John Lubbock, that in many savage races the moral sense is wanting, must be declared a mistake. Over against this we may place the deliberate affirmation of Quatrefages, who has said:—

"Confining ourselves rigorously to the region of facts, and carefully avoiding the territory of philosophy and theology, we may state without hesitation that there is no human society, or even association, in which the idea of good and evil is not represented by certain acts regarded by the members of that society or association as morally good and morally bad. Even among robbers and pirates theft is regarded as a misdeed, sometimes as a crime, and severely punished, while treachery is branded with infamy. The facts noticed by Wallace among the Karubars and Santàls show how the consciousness of moral good and truth is anterior to experience and independent of questions of utility."[1]

Men are not indeed agreed as to what particular actions and feelings should be regarded as good or bad; but this does not affect the present argument, which depends solely on the fact that men universally recognise a distinction in the moral quality of actions.

But not only do all men recognise such a distinction, but also therewith an imperative *obligation* to do whatever they regard as morally right, and not to do what they regard as morally wrong; and, finally, in the heart of every man is heard, so to speak, a voice which signifies approval when he does that which is right, and condemnation when he does that which is wrong; awakening, moreover, an apprehension of retribution as to follow the wrong doing. Let it be carefully observed that our argument is conditioned by no theory as to the origin of these feelings, but simply on the fact that these phenomena universally appear.

[1] "The Human Species," 3d ed. p. 459.

Now it is most significant, that, whether it be possible to reconcile the fact with certain theories or not, it is the special mark of these dicta of conscience, that they never present themselves in consciousness either as originating with the man himself, or as the expression of a law imposed upon him by other men. Rightly or wrongly, they are felt to be the expression of the will of a Power above the individual, and above all men, to which every individual stands related, by no choice of his own, but by a necessity of his nature. And thus it is that the conscience, as a faculty belonging to man's nature, becomes a factor in the origin of religion. Man is religious in virtue of his nature as a moral being.

One other phenomenon, scarcely less significant, claims our notice. Everywhere and always it is to be observed that man craves fellowship with the Being or beings, the God or gods, in whose existence he is constrained to believe. To this fact every form of religion bears witness, and in its teaching and practice has in some way or other given it expression.

Thus religion arises out of man's nature as a spiritual being.

All these facts, then, man's sense of dependence, the laws which determine his thought, the phenomena of conscience, his craving after fellowship with that Power to which he believes himself to be thus mysteriously related,—all are practically universal, and demonstrably independent, as regards their origin, of either education or culture. By this, indeed, it is not intended that all men have consciously reasoned their way from such premises to the belief in a supernatural Power or powers, or that they, if asked, could formulate the subjective process of which such belief, and all religion, is the manifested result. But it is meant that this recognition of an invisible, supernatural Power which is common to religion, everywhere and always, so inevitably arises out of the ordinary experiences of man, that practically this belief is universal.

But if this be true, then we are warranted in affirming that religion must have its origin, subjectively considered, in the very constitution of human nature. Man is religious simply because he is so constituted that for him to be religious is natural, and to be irreligious or non-religious is contra-natural. For in the whole kingdom of life, whatever we find all the individuals of any class, under normal conditions, habitually desiring or doing, we rightly account for such habits by saying that they are due to the constitution of the nature of that order of beings. If the ox everywhere and always eats the green thing of the earth, this is because it is his nature. If the duck everywhere and always seeks the water, this is because this is its nature. So as to the origin of religion. If the subjective phenomena which have been reviewed are universal, and have universally given rise to religion, and have found in various religions of men a more or less perfect expression, evidently we are justified in saying, as in the case of the other illustrations given, that religion must have its origin in the nature of man. He is so constituted that, normally, he is a religious being, just as he is so constituted that, normally, he is a rational being. This fact incontrovertibly distinguishes man even from all those higher orders of the animal kingdom to which, zoölogically, he is most nearly related. Quatrefages is right in saying that the religious and moral phenomena which we see in man, "*isolate*" him from animals.[1] Never has even the most intelligent chimpanzee shown any sign of a tendency to animism or fetish-worship, or made a god out of some dead monkey gone before him, or been discovered clasping his hands in adoration of the rising sun. That men of such standing as the learned Hibbert Lecturer should deny that man has any religious faculty which distinguishes him from the brute, is difficult indeed to understand. It is a striking illustration of the influence which a false philosophy, when accepted, may have, in blinding even a learned and honest man to facts which are irreconcilable with it. None

---

[1] "The Human Species." 3d ed. p. 459. So Reville: "A people absolutely destitute of any religious notion has never been discovered." — "Prolegomena of the History of Religions," translated from the French by A. S. Squire, 1884, p. 201.

the less confidently, because of such denials, may we affirm that man, unlike the brutes, is religious in virtue of the constitution of his nature.

Nevertheless, it has often been strenuously insisted, as in unanswerable contradiction to this affirmation, that not merely individuals, but whole races and tribes of men exist, who exhibit no evidence of any religious belief, feeling, or action. Sir John Lubbock, as is well known, has instanced many such supposed cases in his "Prehistoric Times," and many other writers of eminence have repeated his assertions. Reference has been made to this allegation in a former lecture, but the importance of the question is such that these statements deserve a fuller notice at this point.

In many instances where investigators have declared that no form of religion existed, the term "religion" has been evidently employed in a very restricted sense, applicable only to its higher forms. Hence because in this or that tribe some have not discovered anything which corresponded to their own elevated conception of religion, they have—correctly enough, in the sense in which they used the term—denied in these cases its existence. With a more correct conception as to what alone are the essential elements in religion, there is no doubt that many of such statements would never have been made.

It is, again, of great importance to observe the fact that it is exceedingly difficult for foreigners, even when they have resided for some time among a barbarous people,—and very much more so for a casual traveller,—to gain accurate information as to their religious beliefs. As a general rule, such peoples are disinclined to profane—as they imagine—their religious beliefs and practices by disclosing them freely to strangers and aliens. Then, again, the forms in which the religious beliefs and feelings of degraded savage races are expressed, are often so entirely different from anything of the kind familiar to the foreigner, that even when their religious rites are observed, he fails to recognise their real character. Still further, even in cases where he has so far gained the confidence of the people as to overcome their natural reluctance to speak to him of such matters, there remains the great difficulty of language. The foreigner uses terms in one sense; they, in another; so that it is often only by the exercise of the greatest skill, ingenuity, and patience, that one succeeds in ascertaining the real beliefs of those to whom he is speaking.

Finally, it is to be observed that in many cases where earlier investigators have reported that no religion existed, subsequent and more prolonged and careful inquiry and observation have shown such statements to be incorrect. This has occurred so often, that even if a few cases remain in which such assertions are still made without positive disproval, the presumption becomes very strong that further research would disclose the existence of religious beliefs and actions in these cases also.[1]

---

[1] So Tiele: "No tribe or nation has yet been met with destitute of belief in any higher beings; and travellers who asserted their existence have been afterwards refuted by the facts." — "Outlines of the History of Religion," p. 6.

But it is again objected, that whatever may be said as to races and tribes of men, it must be admitted that many individuals in all races have been sincere atheists; whence it is urged that however common belief in a supernatural Power or powers may be, it cannot be due to the constitution of our nature; but must instead have arisen from tradition, education, or some unknown adventitious cause.

In reply to this, attention may be called first to the fact that the term "atheist," in its most usual application, denotes only those who deny the existence of a personal God, such as the Jewish, Christian, and Mohammedan Scriptures describe. But obviously, it is quite possible that a man may deny the existence of such a Being, and yet admit, as very many do, the existence of a Power or powers invisible, by which his destiny is determined; and also, that his feeling and actions may be determined by that belief. Such, in fact, appears to be the position of many who in our day are called agnostics, as also it is that of pantheists and of orthodox Buddhists. Hence it is evident that such persons cannot be rightly regarded as exceptions to the statement that religion, in the sense in which the term is used in these lectures. is universal.

In the second place, even the fact that, besides these, some men are atheists in the strict sense of the word, cannot be justly held to disprove the truth of the affirmation of the universality of religion. There are not a few in the world who are idiots and lunatics; but no one would think of urging this fact as disproving the truth of the proposition that man is a rational being in virtue of his nature. Instances of genuine and sincere atheism are so few that they must be regarded as abnormal exceptions to the rule which is practically universal, that man is a religious being.

It is, again, of decisive significance that there is no evidence that atheism is ever an original phenomenon, or that it belongs to a very early stage of human development, as that which is natural to man, antecedent to reflection, or to the influences of education and culture. On the contrary, atheism appears most frequently among the most highly cultivated of our race, with whom it is often the result of an ineffectual effort to resolve the profound moral and metaphysical difficulties which are confessedly involved in the affirmation of an almighty personal God; while, in other cases, again, one cannot close the eyes to the fact that atheism is loudly proclaimed by men who are evidently resolutely given to courses of life which must inevitably predispose them to silence, or as far as possible ignore, the witness of conscience and the testimony of nature to the existence of a Power which is governing the world on principles of moral law. In any case, as Quatrefages, again, has said, "we nowhere meet with atheism except in an erratic condition. In every place, and at all times, the mass of populations have escaped it."[1]

Still less is it inconsistent with the affirmation of the universality of religion, that a large part of the human race, engrossed in the eager pursuit of various earthly goods, are quite oblivious of the existence of any supernatural

[1] "The Human Species," pp. 482, 483.

Power, or of their relation to such Power; any more than when we see now and then instances of unnatural parents, we regard this as forbidding the affirmation that affection for one's offspring is an attribute which belongs to the nature of man. To determine that which belongs to the nature of any creature by exceptional deviations from ordinary phenomena, is most unscientific. That which is natural in man's bodily life is not studied to the best advantage in a hospital.

In the light of all the facts, therefore, we need not hesitate, on account of such instances, to affirm that religion is so universal that it must have its origin, on the subjective side, in the constitution of human nature. Religion exists because man is what he is; because he is naturally and normally led to regard himself and the universe in which he finds himself, as dependent on an invisible Power or powers, superior to himself and all that he sees about him, with which Power or powers he feels an instinctive craving to be on terms of friendship and fellowship.

Man, then, by nature, has a faculty or capacity for religion. Yet that alone would not account for religion. A man may have eyes, but as long as he is shut up in a dark cave, he cannot see. So a man might have a faculty of apprehending God and his relation to Him, but without a revelation of Him he could not have a religion. The phenomena which are presented in the existence and the history of religion would be still inexplicable, except we assume, not merely a natural capacity in man for forming religious conceptions, but also, correlated with these, a revelation of God to man, both original and universal. It is not indeed necessary, in order to account for the facts, to suppose that such a revelation must have been given in a supernatural manner. Even Holy Scripture does not so represent the case.[1] But an objective revelation, in some way, of the existence, and to some extent, of the character, of God, there must have been from the beginning, or the phenomena presented in religion are unaccountable.

[1] See *e.g.* Ps. xix. and Rom. i. 20.

For the fundamental religious beliefs of men are marked by four characteristics; namely, spontaneity, universality, great intensity, and invincible persistency; and for each and all of these, any theory of the origin of religion must be required to account, in order to its own vindication. If there has never been an objective revelation of the existence of any such Power as religious faith assumes, these characteristics of religious belief are all utterly inexplicable.

It has indeed been often objected that the wide acceptance of Buddhism forbids the affirmation that these four characteristics are essential to religion. This is supposed to disprove the assertion that religious belief, as defined in these lectures, is either spontaneous or invincibly persistent.

But the objection will not bear close examination in the light of history. On the contrary, the history of Buddhism is one of the most impressive illustrations possible of those very characteristics of religious belief which it is supposed by some to disprove. It is indeed true that according to the earliest Buddhist authorities, the Buddha appears not indeed to have denied, but certainly to have ignored, the existence of a personal God, the First Cause and Moral Governor of the world. Yet, even so, he was not able to leave wholly out of his system the Hindoo conception of supernatural beings called gods. These were not indeed represented by him as creators or rulers of the world, but they were nevertheless supernatural beings, living and acting in a higher sphere than that of men; and in admitting these, even though only in the way of tolerance, into a subordinate place in his religious system, the Buddha made a most significant concession to the imperative demands of man's religious nature. But this did not suffice to satisfy the cravings of the human heart; and so it followed that the Northern Buddhism, most fully developed in Thibet, despite the authority of the Buddha, elaborated its remarkable conception of an Ádi Buddha, eternal, almighty, self-existent, the Author of all being, and thereby furnished one of the most decisive proofs which history affords, of the invincible persistency of man's belief in the existence of a supernatural Power, the Cause of the existence of man and of all things.

Affirming, then, the four characteristics of religious beliefs above named, we argue that these are unaccountable except there has been, and is, a veritable revelation of a God. This is necessary to account for the spontaneity and universality of religion. It is of course quite true that there is much in the religious belief and practices of different peoples which is not spontaneous, as it is not universal; and which may be sufficiently explained by the influence of tradition, or example, or education. But when we eliminate all such beliefs and observances, and regard simply that fundamental belief in the existence of a supernatural Power or powers to which man stands mysteriously related, which is common to all religions; of this common conviction, it is certain that neither tradition, nor the presence or the absence of education or culture, can afford an adequate explanation.

THE TRUE GENESIS OF RELIGION. 175

These beliefs, as has been shown, appear antecedent to and independent of argument, alike among the most debased savages, and the most highly cultivated of our race, no less in the most modern than in the most ancient times. Even if we grant that in experience men derive their first religious beliefs from the instruction and example of their immediate parents, it is obvious that instruction and example would fail us as an explanation of the origin of religious beliefs in the case of the first man or men. In these, we must assume the belief to have spontaneously arisen. For religious belief, in the first instance, either there was an adequate ground, in a real objective revelation of the existence of a God, and of man's relation to him, or there was not. It is indeed possible for a man to affirm the latter alternative, and assume that the belief, however it may have arisen out of the nature of the first men, was the result of their extremely ignorant and semi-bestial condition. But if this were so, then as men increased in intelligence, the belief ought to tend to disappear; which, however, is contrary to the fact.

Finally, if in the face of the admitted phenomena of religious belief, the inference of an objective revelation of a God be denied, this denial carries with it into every department of human thought the most destructive consequences. For it is certain that religious belief, once originated, has proved one of the strongest and most ineradicable of all human convictions. It would be impossible to instance any belief common to mankind, which has everywhere and always so powerfully affected human action. It has often prompted individuals and whole nations and ranks of men to the most intense and long-continued labours, to the voluntary endurance of prolonged, and often very terrible, hardships and sufferings. It is not too much to say that the art, the literature, and the politics of the world have been more universally and profoundly affected, both directly and indirectly, by the religious convictions of men, than by any other beliefs held in common by the race.

And the persistency of these beliefs has corresponded with their intensity. Never, either among the most degraded or the most civilised peoples, has atheism for any time remained the professed belief of even a small part of our race. Even when, in individual communities, as in France at the close of the last century, it has seemed as if now religious belief were about destroyed, it has never been possible to eradicate it; and repeatedly, after such temporary decline of its vigour, it has reasserted itself with renewed intensity.

Now if, notwithstanding this spontaneity, universality, intensity, and persistency of religious belief, we assume that there neither is, nor has been at any time, any revelation to man of the existence of such a Power as religious faith assumes, what then? Evidently there is but one alternative left us. If for religious belief there is no such objective ground, then it follows that man is so constituted that, with very rare exceptions, he spontaneously believes, and that with the greatest intensity and tenacity of conviction, what is false; and this in reference to the most momentous matter which can possibly come before his mind. But if this be the fact in respect to man's universal, spontaneous, and so persistent belief on this point, it must be granted as quite possible that he should also be mistaken in any or all other similar spontaneous and persistent beliefs. But if this be possible, then, since all knowledge is conditioned ultimately on the assumption of the trustworthiness of our spontaneous and necessary beliefs, how can we escape the logical conclusion that certitude on any subject is unattainable? From this so destructive and fatal conclusion there is no escape, except by assuming that the fundamental religious beliefs of man have been determined by the fact of an actual revelation, in some way, and in some measure, of the existence and nature of such a Power as religion contemplates.

And we shall only agree with the great majority of mankind, even of its most profound and illustrious thinkers, when we affirm that such a revelation, which we are obliged to postulate, in order to account for the phenomena presented by religion, is a perpetual fact. To exhibit this at length, the limits of this lecture forbid. We can only touch upon the subject. In the first place, conscience, of which we have spoken as a faculty, also involves a revelation of God; even though it be often obscured to the consciousness, by inattention, prejudice, and sin. For the phenomena of conscience are not only a manifestation of the nature of man, as a being capable of recognising moral law and religious obligation, but, inseparably from this, they also manifest a Being above man, whose will, so far as made known, man, whether it be pleasing to him or not, whether it seem to his present worldly advantage or not, is under an irremovable obligation to obey. For whenever a man does what is wrong, and then instinctively shrinks with dread from the future, lest somewhere in that future he shall meet with retribution for that wrong doing, he thereby in no ambiguous way confesses that he thinks that he perceives, even through the obscurity of this earthly life, a Power which will hold him responsible for that breach of law; a Power from whose reach even death shall not certainly enable him to escape. Thus it follows that from the very beginning of his moral activity, man must have been brought face to face, in the spontaneous operations of his conscience, with a revelation, more or less clear, of the being and will of God; a revelation which was also a revelation of his character, in so far at least as this, that He must be a moral Being and the absolute Ruler of all men.

But the external world has also ever been to man a revelation of the existence of a Power above man, and above all nature. Never, except in rare and erratic cases, have men been able to believe that the sensible world was its own sufficient cause and explanation. To say no more, man cannot well help seeing that the universe reveals a Power which, even if it be immanent in the universe, as it is, is yet in so far distinct from it that in some way the universe must be its product and effect. Even such an extreme evolutionist as Reville is willing in this sense to admit that the phenomena of religion require us to believe that God has revealed himself to man; and that man " was so constituted that, arrived at a certain stage in his psychical development, he must become sensible of the reality of the Divine influence. " In this sense," he says, "which leaves perfect freedom to history, we also could accept the idea of a primitive revelation."[1]

We find, then, the origin of religion in these two factors: the one, subjective, the other, objective; the former. the constitution of man's nature, in virtue of which he necessarily believes in the existence of a Power invisible and supernatural, to which he stands necessarily related; the latter, in the actual revelation of such a Power in the phenomena of conscience, and in the physical universe without us.

[1] " Prolegomena," etc., p. 36.

LECTURE VI.

THE DEVELOPMENT OF RELIGION: SIN AS A FACTOR.

THE history of religion undoubtedly presents us with an evolution, as the popular modern phrase is. Religions have not arisen suddenly and independently of what had gone before. It is true of religious history, as of all history, that the roots of the present are in the past, as those of each past, in a yet earlier past. In many instances, we are able to trace the genesis of a religion out of a preceding religion, historically; as in the rise of Buddhism out of the earlier Brahmanism, or of Muhammedanism out of Christianity and Judaism. Nor is Christianity an exception to this law. Though it was, in one sense, a new religion, supernaturally introduced through the incarnation, life, death, and resurrection, of the Son of God, it was yet so related to the antecedent Judaism as without it to have been impossible. The affirmation of a supernatural factor in Judaism or Christianity in no wise requires us to ignore or deny the co-operation of natural causes also, in their origination and development, any more than the recognition of the natural causes involves, as some seem to suppose, the denial of the supernatural factor.

Again, in every religion, when it has been once established, we observe a progressive development. No religion has ever remained, in the apprehension and practice of those who profess it, exactly what it was in its beginning. Religions are modified as the years and centuries go by, whether in the way of elevation and progress, or, on the other hand, of regress and degradation. It takes little careful reading to discover in the Christian Scriptures, historically regarded, a very manifest progress in the development of doctrine. Only a school of interpretation, now about extinct, will seek to discover everything in Genesis which appears in the Gospels or Apocalypse. The theology of Genesis is very simple and elementary, as compared even with that of the prophets; and when it is compared with any of the New Testament books, the contrast is still more obvious.

This fact is now so commonly recognised by intelligent Christians, that it might seem superfluous to remark it, except that many of the chief authorities who have written of late years on the history of religion, have so unaccountably misapprehended, and hence misrepresented, the belief of intelligent evangelical Christians on this point; assuming that because such maintain that man began his history with a true knowledge of the one living God, they also have intended therein to affirm that the first men enjoyed a full knowledge of all those truths which are now the possession of the church.

A striking illustration of this is found in Reville's "Prolegomena to a History of Religion," in which the learned author, contending against the Christian doctrine of a primeval supernatural revelation, urges that "it is infinitely hard to imagine that in the beginning of his slow and painful development, man, yet plunged in absolute ignorance, was in possession of sublime religious doctrines, such as the most pure inspiration has been able to offer to a cultivated society, rich in accumulated experience." From which he concludes that " the hypothesis of a primeval revelation of religious truth is in contradiction to all that we know as to the extremely miserable and uncultured state of humanity anterior to history."[1] To which argument it is sufficient to say in reply, that no intelligent Christian holds any such extravagant belief as to the degree of knowledge of God which was possessed by our first parents as Reville supposes; nor does the record in Genesis, which such accept as authoritative, so represent their condition.

In view of modern controversies, it is, however, important to emphasise the remark that it does not follow that because the religious beliefs of the first men were few and elementary, therefore they must have been erroneous. It does not follow from this admission, that before man could have attained a knowledge

[1] "Prolegomena," etc., p. 40.

of the one true God, he must have been a worshipper of nature, or of fetishes, or of shadows or ghosts. As in all other matters of human knowledge, so in religion, it is quite possible that although a man may know very little, he may know that little very accurately.

We may then at once admit, subject only to these necessary explanations, that in every religion is to be observed a growth or development. And so the question arises, What has been the usual order of that development? Admitting that man is religious in virtue of the constitution of his nature, so that from the first he must have had some religious belief; admitting, moreover, that the primitive religious belief must have been most simple and elementary, what was the character of that original faith of men? Was it monotheism, or was it something else? some form of polytheism, dualism, nature-worship, fetish or spirit-worship? Of these, which is primary, and which are secondary?

Professor Max Müller, indeed, as also Reville, strangely insists that this is "an idle question."[1] The latter tells us that primitive humanity was "incapable of making any such distinction."[2] But such an assertion, even if true, cannot be proved, till some one shall have produced some decisive evidence that the first man was such a semi-bestial being as it assumes him to have been. For to say that primeval man was not capable of knowing whether he worshipped one God, or more than one, is to place him lower in the scale of intelligence than many brutes. It is said to have been shown by a curious experiment, that even the crow can count up to three. A creature, even though having the bodily form of an adult man, who could not distinguish between one and two, either would not be a man; or, if a man, an idiot. But all the evidence shows that the earliest men whose remains have been discovered were as far from being such idiots as we are. The so-called "Calaveras skull," for instance, according to the eminent geologist, Professor Wright, "is in no sense ape-

---

[1] "Chips from a German Workshop," vol. i, pp. 27, 28.
[2] "Prolegomena," etc., p. 61.

like in character, but may well have contained the brain of a philosopher."[1]

It is not therefore "an idle question" whether or not monotheism is primitive. We cannot fairly decline to face the question: Was monotheism the starting-point, or must we regard it as the goal of the religious development of man? Are henotheism, polytheism, etc., to be regarded as successive stadia in the progress of man toward the recognition of one personal God and Father in Heaven? or, on the contrary, do these mark successive stages of departure and decline from a pure primitive faith in one personal God?

Reville asserts the former alternative, declaring dogmatically that "we cannot deny the original polytheism";[2] and with him substantially agree the whole school of naturalistic evolutionists. But this denial of an original monotheism, as before remarked, proceeds from the assumption that man was developed by slow and

---

[1] "Bibliotheca Sacra," April, 1891, article, *Recent Discoveries bearing on the Antiquity of Man.*
[2] "Prolegomena," etc., p. 61.

insensible degrees from the condition of an irrational brute; a theory which such an unprejudiced scientist as Virchow declares to be not yet established, and which Alfred Russell Wallace even declares to be irreconcilable with certain indisputable facts. Whether, apart from the argument derived from this mistaken assumption, there is independent evidence for the gradual evolution of monotheism, we shall see in the sequel.

The question of the nature of the religion of the primitive man is one which cannot be historically determined by direct testimony. We can only arrive at a decision of this question by way of inference from facts at present known. But such a method is capable of at least conducting us to a conclusion which shall have a high degree of probability. If, in historical investigation, the further back we go, the more, as a general rule, we find monotheism disappearing, and the lower forms of religious faith, such as the worship of fetishes, of ancestors, or of nature, becoming more and more prominent, then certainly such facts would tend to show that the opinion of those who maintain that monotheism could not have been the original form of religion, was probably correct. But if, on the contrary, in those cases in which we can trace the history of religion, we either find a monotheistic faith more and more prominent, the more remote the antiquity to which we ascend; or if, again, in the case of other races, although the earliest records reveal no trace of monotheistic belief, we yet find, as the centuries roll by, no tendency to develop it, then certainly we shall rightly assume that monotheism is, far more probably, the earliest form of religious belief, of which all others are more or less extreme degenerations. For it is clearly in the last degree unlikely that the direction of development in prehistoric times should have been the reverse of that exhibited in the historic period; and we may with full confidence argue from any law revealed as operating in the latter, to the existence of the same law in the former period. That the facts sustain the latter of the two alternatives supposed, we shall see abundant reason to believe.

Inasmuch as in this inquiry we have no historic records which bring us within thousands of years of the beginning of human life, it is evident that the question of the antecedent probability becomes of more than ordinary importance and argumentative value. The whole naturalistic school of evolutionist writers on religion are wont to assume that the antecedent probability is decisive against the possibility of an original monotheism; and if their naturalistic theories as to the origin of man be granted, in this they are certainly right. For if man was evolved out of the brute in such a purely natural and gradual manner as they assume, it would plainly be most difficult to indicate the precise point in his ascent where this developing creature became a man, and an original monotheism would be almost inconceivable. But for reasons already fully given, we cannot admit the right to take this assumption for granted, or allow that upon the disputed hypothesis of a purely *naturalistic* evolution, any argument as to the nature of man's earliest religion, or as to the order of religious development, can rightly be based.

Not only so, but we affirm that the phenomena connected with man's consciousness of sin are such as to establish a weighty probability in favour of the opposite view; namely, that monotheism must be presumed to have been the original type of religious belief, of which all others must be regarded as variously degraded forms.

It is one of the most remarkable characteristics of modern naturalistic theories of the development of religion, that, for the most part, they ignore this universal consciousness of sin, and quietly assume that religious development has progressed under normal conditions, and thus also must have been marked, on the whole, by a progressive elevation and continuous improvement of man's religious ideas. But this common assumption is in contradiction to most manifest and indisputable facts. Conscience in all ages has steadily witnessed that man's moral relation to the Power with whom in religion he has to do, is not what it should be. All religions agree in taking it for granted that in this relation there is something abnormal.

which, somehow, through religion, needs, if possible, to be set right. In a word, they testify, always and everywhere, that man feels himself to be a sinner, and, because of this, out of harmony with the Power which rules the universe. About this fact there is no room for debate. One may, if he will, regard this universal feeling as a groundless superstition. But such an individual opinion cannot remove the fact that, as a rule, the great mass of men, and the noblest, purest natures and deepest thinkers, most of all, have sadly recognised a moral disharmony between themselves and that mysterious Power which conscience discerns in nature.

The truth of this general statement is not affected, nor its significance in the present argument lessened, because in some individuals this consciousness of sin appears to be extinct. For it is one of the most constantly observed effects of continued sin, that it tends to produce a certain numbness and deadness of the moral sense. The only wonder is that individuals who have no sense of sin, are not more common than they are.

Neither is the bearing of this fact on the question before us affected by the circumstance that very great differences of belief are found among men, as to what specific acts or feelings are to be regarded as sin. For this difference only concerns the question as to what are those particular moral acts or states, because of which the disharmony between man and the Unseen Power exists. All alike, however they may differ on this point, assume the fact that the disharmony exists.

Now it is no exaggeration to say that this consciousness of sin and guilt has been one of the most potent factors in the development of religion. Practically, the religions of the world have addressed themselves chiefly to the problems presented by the fact of sin, and the pain and sorrow which is commonly perceived to be a consequence of sin. Hence, to write a history, or elaborate a theory, of the development of religion, and either ignore the phenomena presented in the consciousness of sin, or assign them an influence subordinate and insignificant, thus assuming that the development of religion has been essentially normal, is utterly unscientific. Such an assumption can only lead to a misreading of facts, and, in consequence, to erroneous conclusions. He who makes such an assumption, and interprets facts accordingly, commits an error no less fatal to any correct result than that of the student who should attempt to construct a theory of physiology, solely from data presented by diseased persons, mistakenly supposed by him to be sound and well.

And yet a no less eminent specialist in this subject than M. Reville, introduces into the foundation of his argument this very assumption; representing it as inconceivable that the history of the development of religion should be "nothing more than an exposition of the degradation and corruption of moral truth." What is this but to assume that man, who is everywhere presented to our observation as morally sick, is morally well? Incredible, indeed, such a

[1] "Prolegomena," etc., p. 35.

record of a continual tendency to the degradation of religion would appear, if man's moral condition were normal; but how, if it be abnormal? What shall we say, if we regard the testimony of conscience, that man is suffering universally from a profound constitutional disorder of his moral and spiritual nature? If this be true, then is it not rather inconceivable that the history of religion should not bear witness to a no less universal tendency to moral and spiritual degradation and corruption?

For it is undeniable that sin universally and constantly tends to modify a man's religious beliefs and feelings for the worse. It ever tends to dull to the consciousness, the voice of conscience, which affirms a moral law, and therewith a personal Lawgiver, not many, but One and Supreme.

Sin also begets fear, and the more that the consciousness of sin is developed, ever more and more fear. Sin also is ever manifested in desire for that which the fleshly lower nature of man craves, but the moral law condemns. How natural, then, how inevitable, indeed, that sin should powerfully influence the development of religion; as inclining men always to wrong views of the nature and character of God! How natural that we should see — as we do see — many religions which express little else than the consciousness of fear and dread; dread of a great God, or gods, on high, or of malign unseen powers resident in nature! How evident, again. that, because the consciousness of sin awakens fear of retribution from the unseen Power against whom man has sinned, therefore, inasmuch as fear is painful, men will be unfailingly predisposed to look with favour upon such views of God, or of the world, or of both, as, if assumed to be true, diminish or remove the ground for fear! How natural thus that men should ever be inclined to imagine gods like unto themselves, who therefore, as themselves unholy, are not greatly displeased with the sinfulness of man!

Hence we find many ready to accept an atheistic or agnostic system, like the early Buddhism or Chinese Confucianism; many more accepting pantheism, as in ancient Egypt, Babylon, and, above all, in India, ancient and modern. For in the former case, if a man can accept an atheistic or an agnostic creed, he practically rids himself of the oppressive belief in an almighty Being, personal and holy, and therefore to be feared by a sinner. In the case of pantheism, the same stupefaction of the warning conscience is secured, both logically and historically, in the highest degree. For in ascribing all human acts, in the same sense, to God, pantheism denies His absolute holiness, as in eternal antagonism to man's sin; reducing sin to a necessary, but transient, moment in the evolutionary process of the one only Being; and by denying free-agency, and by affirming necessity as the law of human life, it consistently shows that no man is responsible for his wrong doing; a doctrine which is repeatedly affirmed as dogma in the sacred books of India. Remembering these things, it is easy to understand why pantheism should have been accepted by such a very large proportion of the human family as the essential truth of religion. Pantheism is to the pangs of conscience what morphine is to aching nerves.

Polytheistic religions — often based, consciously or unconsciously, on pantheistic assumptions — have the same effect of dulling the sense of sin. They do this by lowering the character of God, through representing Him by unworthy symbols; so that as the symbolism becomes progressively more and more degraded, the moral antagonism between man and God is more and more obscured to consciousness.

Finally, sin ever tends to affect for evil the religious development of man, because it lies in the nature of sin, that it tends to the debasement of moral ideals, and so makes it ever more and more easy for man to imagine a god like unto himself.

To all this it is indeed sometimes replied. that, even granting these facts as to man's present sinful condition, and also that sin must modify the religious development, it might nevertheless be true that man naturally tends, as the ages pass, to grow morally better; so that a progressive elevation of man's religious conceptions, in the way of a merely natural development, might still be quite possible. Upon this assumption, sin would be like certain bodily diseases, which run a definite and self-limited course, and which naturally tend to the re-establishment of health.

But however pleasing such a belief would be, the facts of history forbid us to take this optimistic view. As regards the individual, there is nothing clearer than the fact that the natural tendency of a sinner is not toward moral and spiritual improvement, but the reverse. Every man who really struggles in earnest against sin, just in proportion to the strength of the determination of his will against it, finds that the tendency of his nature is ever against him. But if this be true of every individual, how can it but be true of the whole race, which is made up exclusively of such individuals?

And that indeed it is so with the race, all history bears accordant witness. Not only has the natural tendency been downward and not upward, outside of the influence of Judaism and

Christianity, but even Jewish and Christian history furnishes many humiliating illustrations of this law of tendency to moral depravation.

If, now, this be a correct account of the chief phenomena presented in the universal consciousness of sin, it is easy to see on which side the presumption must lie, as regards the order of religious development. That man should have begun with some low and erroneous form of religious belief, and then, being the sinner that he is, through a merely natural development, and apart from any supernatural grace, should have gradually approximated, or at last attained to, the purity of monotheistic faith, as represented in Judaism or Christianity, appears in this light to be nothing less than a wholly incredible hypothesis. A presumption of overwhelming force is therefore established that the natural order of the development of religion cannot have been from animism, fetishism, nature or ancestor worship, upwards, toward the recognition and worship of the one living and true God; but that instead, the religious movement, on lines of nature, must have been from an original monotheism, downwards, along various lines of progressive debasement of the idea of God and of man's relation to Him. Whether the facts of history, so far as ascertainable, are such as this presumption would lead us to anticipate, we have to inquire in the next lecture.

LECTURE VII.

HISTORIC FACTS REGARDING THE ORDER OF RELIGIOUS DEVELOPMENT.

IN the previous lecture it was shown that the phenomena which are exhibited in connection with man's consciousness of sin, are such as to establish the strongest possible presumption against the probability of a gradual improvement and elevation of religion through any forces resident in humanity; so that it is in the last degree unlikely that the order of religious development should have been from an original and primitive worship of spirits, or of fetishes, or of nature, upwards, toward monotheism, and not rather the reverse. We have next to inquire whether or not historical facts, so far as known, are such as to sustain this presumption, and so support the hypothesis that the original form of religious faith must have been monotheistic.

We may well begin the inquiry with the order of development in ancient Egypt. The beginnings of Egyptian history are still veiled in mystery, but we shall doubtless be safe if we assume that the first dynasty of the Egyptian monarchy cannot be placed at a date more recent than about 3400 B.C.; not forgetting that some eminent scholars insist on a date one or two thousand years earlier.[1] On the assumption of 3400 B.C. as the lowest possible date, we then have a literature covering a minimum period of about three thousand years, ending with the early Christian centuries. The time is certainly sufficiently long to enable us to judge of the general religious tendency of the people; and as, fortunately, the literature and other monuments of Egypt are not only very abundant, but have much to say regarding

[1] Renouf says: "The date of the Great Pyramid cannot be more recent than 3000 B.C." But this is not yet the beginning of the long series of Egyptian dynasties; and there appears also to be sufficient evidence that man existed in the Nile valley long before the first dynasty. See "The Origin and Growth of Religion as illustrated by the Religion of Ancient Egypt," by M. Le Page Renouf (Hibbert Lectures for 1879), p. 50.

religious matters, the data for forming an intelligent judgment are all that we could ask.

From this literature it appears that both monotheism and polytheism coexisted in Egypt from the time of the earliest records. Illustrations of the latter need not be adduced. Every one is familiar with the gross idolatry of ancient Egypt, their worship of sacred bulls, and cats, and crocodiles; of leeks and onions; of sun, and moon, and stars. But those who have not looked into the matter may well be surprised to find also in this literature, declarations of the moral character of God, as the sole, supreme Ruler of heaven and earth, which in many instances might be used without modification to express the belief of the Christian.

Thus in the "Maxims of Ptahhotep," the most ancient book in the world, dating from the time of the pyramid-builders, we find such passages as these:—

"If any one beareth himself proudly, he will be humbled by God, who maketh his strength."

"If thou art a wise man, bring up thy son in the love of God."

"God loveth the obedient, and hateth the disobedient."[1]

In the Maxims of Ani we read:—

"Pray humbly with a loving heart, all the words of which are uttered in secret: He (God) will protect thee in thy affairs; He will listen to thy words."

"Give thyself to God; keep thyself continually for God, and let to-morrow be like to-day. Let thine eyes consider the acts of God; it is He who smiteth him that is smitten."[2]

This "God" of whom Ptahhotep and Ani speak, is described even as in the Christian Scriptures, as "the great God, Lord of heaven and of earth, who made all things which are."[3] And to this God the prayer is offered:—

"O my God and Lord, who hast made me,

---

[1] Quoted by Renouf, "Origin and Growth of Religion," etc., pp. 100, 101.

[2] Ib. pp. 102, 103. [3] Ib. p. 216.

and formed me, give me an eye to see and an ear to hear thy glories."[1]

Such expressions, which are exceedingly numerous, amply justify the strong language of Rougé, quoted by Renouf: "The first characteristic of the (Egyptian) religion is the unity (of God) most energetically expressed; God, one, sole. and only ; no others with Him. . . . He has made everything, and He alone has not been made."[2]

This understanding of these ancient testimonies concerning the religion of ancient Egypt is sustained by Renouf. who, commenting on some of the above-cited texts, uses these words : —

"There can, I trust, be no doubt, who that power is which, in our translations, we do not hesitate to call God. It is unquestionably the true and only God. who is not far from any of us; for in Him we live, and move, and have our being; whose ' eternal power and godhead' and government of the world were made

[1] Quoted by Renouf, "Origin and Growth of Religion," etc., p. 216.   [2] Ib. p. 89.

known through that Light which enlighteneth every man that cometh into the world."[1]

The writings of ancient Egypt thus witness not only to the existence of polytheism in ancient Egypt, but, no less clearly, to the coexistence with it of a high type of monotheistic belief. Now the question vital to the present argument is evidently this: What, according to these ancient authorities, is the relation of time and succession in which the Egyptian monotheism and polytheism stand to each other? According to any evolutionary theory of religion, we ought to find the nature-worship in its various forms, most prominent in the earliest literature; and then, coming down the centuries, we should be able to observe a gradual evolution of monotheism out of that earlier faith. Is this, in fact, what we do find? Let us again hear one of the high authorities already cited. Referring to the monotheistic element in Egyptian literature, Renouf says: —

"It is incontestably true that the sublimer

---

[1] Quoted by Renouf, "Origin and Growth of Religion," etc., p. 103.

portions of the Egyptian religion are not the comparatively late result of a process of development, of elimination from the grosser. The sublimer portions are demonstrably ancient; and the last stage of the Egyptian religion . . . was by far the grossest and most corrupt." [1]

Rougé, whom Renouf quotes, agrees with him in asserting this same order as historical fact. He says:—

"More than five thousand years since, in the valley of the Nile, the hymn began to the Unity of God and the immortality of the soul, and we find Egypt in the last ages arrived at the most unbridled polytheism. The belief in the Unity of the Supreme God and in His attributes as Creator and Law-giver of man, . . . these are the primitive notions, encased like indestructible diamonds in the midst of the mythological superfetations accumulated in the centuries which have passed over that ancient civilisation." [2]

The facts thus show that the order of the

[1] "Origin and Growth of Religion," etc., p. 91. See also p. 249.   [2] Quoted ib., p. 91.

development of religion in Egypt was the exact opposite of that which any evolutionary theory of religion would require; but in perfect accord with the presumption established in the previous lecture, on the ground of the observed phenomena connected with man's consciousness of sin. The order of the Egyptian development was not from the lower to the higher forms of religious belief, but the reverse. It is the most ancient Egyptian literature which exhibits the noblest and purest faith. In that of the earlier dynasties we find the doctrines of the unity, personality, and spirituality of God, as the Creator of the world, "strenuously asserted"; although with this we also may observe manifestations of a tendency to religious debasement. The powers of nature were already worshipped; but in that early day they appear to have been regarded merely as the diverse manifestations of the one *Nutar*, or Power, from whom all powers proceed. But by the 19th dynasty, or about the time of the Exodus, the conception of the personality of God, as above and transcending the world He had created, had largely given place to a pantheistic view of God's relation to the world, which then led rapidly on, as always, to the development of a system of nature-worship, and that of a very gross kind; as of cats, and bulls, and crocodiles, and beetles, the ultimate and most degraded stage of the Egyptian religion, as it was chiefly known to the Greek writers, and, still later, to the early Christian fathers.

Similar was the order of development in the religion of India. The most ancient deity, probably, of the Indo-Aryans, was *Dyaus*, called more specifically *Dyaus pitar*, lit. Heaven-Father, the original form, as is well known, of the Latin *Jupiter*, as is *Dyaus* of the Greek *Zeus*, all denoting the Supreme God. But already in the earliest Vedic days, according to Professor Max Müller, *Dyaus pitar* had become "a fading star," and other deities were coming above the horizon, such *Aditi*, "the Infinite Expanse"; *Varuna*, "the Star-lit sky"; *Mithrà*, "the god of day," etc. As time passed on, the number of deities was multiplied more and more; still, however, for the most part, representing natural phenomena. Such were *Indra*, the god of rain; *Vayu*, the god of wind; the *Máruts*, or gods of the storm; *Súrya*, the Sun-god; *Ushas*, the goddess of the dawn; and especially *Agni*, the god of fire, etc.

But in that earliest form of the Indo-Aryan religion, each of these chief deities is addressed as if it were the one only Supreme Being; precisely as in old time were *Osiris*, *Ra*, and other gods of Egypt. Thus *Agni* is said to be "the Lawgiver of the Universe"; *Indra* is declared to be "higher than all"; *Agni*, *Súrya*, *Indra*, and *Vishnu*, are, each alike, styled "king of all gods and men":[1] the phase of religion which Max Müller has called henotheism; and the explanation of which according to the *Rig Veda*, i, 164, is found in the fact that these are all regarded as simply various manifestations of one Divine Being. "They call him *Indra*, *Mithra*, *Varuna*, *Agni*, — that which is One, the wise name by different terms."

Such is the form of religion which

Ebrard, "Apologetik," 2 Bd. § 15.

meets us in the earliest Vedic period. In name, many gods appear, generally impersonations of powers and objects of nature; but these are still regarded, not so much as distinct deities, but rather as various manifestations of a God who is essentially one. Of fetish-worship or ancestor-worship in that early time, we find not a trace, though there is enough of it later. The phenomena of that early Vedic religion have been described, as beautifully as truly, by Professor Max Müller in the following language: "There is a monotheism that precedes the polytheism of the Veda; and even in the invocations of their innumerable gods, the remembrance of a God, one and infinite, breaks through the mist of idolatrous phraseology, like the blue sky that is hidden by passing clouds."[1]

The best spirit of that time is eloquently witnessed by the often-cited Hymn 121 of the 1st *Mandala* of the Rig Veda, a part of which is as follows, the first line being

[1] "History of Sanskrit Literature," p. 559.

repeated as a refrain at the end of each verse: —

> "What God shall we adore with sacrifice?[1]
> Him let us praise, the golden child that rose
> In the beginning, who was born the lord —
> The one sole lord of all that is — who made
> The earth, and formed the sky, who giveth life,
> Who giveth strength, whose bidding gods revere,
> Whose hiding-place is immortality,
> Whose shadow, death; who by his might is king
> Of all the breathing, sleeping, waking world —
> Who governs men and beasts . . . to whom
> Both earth and heaven, established by his will,
> Look up with trembling mind; . . .
> . . . . the only God
> Above the gods. May he not injure us!
> He, the Creator of the earth — the righteous
> Creator of the sky, Creator too
> Of oceans bright, and far extending waters."[2]

Words such as these might then have seemed to give promise of continued progress toward clearer and clearer recognition of the one God and Father in heaven; but so it was not

[1] The words are repeated as a refrain after each line.
[2] As rendered by Sir M. Monier-Williams, in "Indian Wisdom," 2d ed., p. 23.

to be. Even in the Rig Veda appear conceptions which were to develop at last, not into a yet clearer monotheism, but into the most elaborate and consistent system of pantheism which perhaps the world has ever seen. Thus, in a hymn addressed to *Áditi*, we read: —

"*Áditi* is the sky (*Dyaus*); *Áditi* is the air; *Áditi* is the mother and father and son; *Áditi* is the collective gods; *Áditi* is the five persons; *Áditi* is whatever has been born; *Áditi* is whatever is to be born."[1]

In the *Upanishads*, which we may assign to a period immediately following the sixth century B.C., pantheism is fully and explicitly taught, though not always yet with strict consistency. Thus, in the *Bṛihad-áranyaka Upanishad* (II. i. 20), the relation of the universe, visible and invisible, to the Supreme Being, is thus expressed: —

"As the web issues from the spider, as little sparks proceed from fire, so from the one Soul

[1] Quoted by Robson, "Hinduism in its Relation to Christianity," p. 18.

proceed all breathing animals, all worlds, all the gods, and all beings." [1]

In the *Mundaka Upanishad* (I. i. 7) the same thought is expressed thus: —

" As from a blazing fire consubstantial sparks proceed in a thousand ways, so from the imperishable (Spirit) various living souls are produced, and they return to him too." [2]

From this, the logical conclusion is the deification of man, and this was affirmed as truth in the first-named *Upanishad* (IV. 4: 15) as it still is by the millions of orthodox Hindoos. We read: —

" When a person regards his own soul as truly God, as the lord of what was and is to be, then he does not wish to conceal from himself that Soul." [3]

Not yet, however, was the pantheistic doctrine accepted without controversy. Out of these *Upanishads*, arose, five or six centuries before Christ, the so-called *Shad-Darshana*, or " Six Systems " of philosophy, which, as regards our

[1] Quoted by Sir M. Monier-Williams, "Indian Wisdom," p. 39.
[2] Ib. p. 43.   [3] Ib. p. 39.

present subject, may be regarded as three. These all agreed on the following points: namely, that soul, as, also, in respect of its substance, the material universe, is without beginning and without end; that consciousness, with its associated phenomena, is conditioned by the connexion of soul with body, and is maintained in most cases through transmigration. It was also unanimously agreed that this state of things is necessarily evil, and that hence the *summum bonum*, the ultimate end of all things and the highest object of all religion, is the loss of personal self-consciousness, and reabsorption in the one Supreme and only Being, if there be one.[1]

In the *Nyáya* and the closely related *Vaisheshika* system, the material world is regarded as made by the aggregation of atoms. If we ask how the atoms came together, or are parted again, the answer is, not by the power of God, but by the power of *Adrishta*, literally, "the Unseen." In the *Vaisheshika Shástra* God is not named, and in the original

[1] See "Indian Wisdom," lect. iii, pp. 61–70.

Nyáya Shástra but once, and then only incidentally by an objector to the system. In this case the idea of God, all pervasive in Vedic days, had now become a vanishing quantity; though the later *Naiyáyika* writers still strive to retain it, as when in the *Kusmánjali* we read : —

" An omniscient and indestructible Being is to be proved from the existence of effects, from the combination of atoms," etc.[1]

Still, even so, the idea of God was greatly lowered, as the atoms of which the universe is composed, were still assumed to be coeternal with and independent of God.

In the *Sánkhya* the conception of God has disappeared altogether. It is declared that " the existence of a supreme Lord is unproved," and that, " there can be no proof of his existence "; and that, even if he did exist, " he could not be effective of any creation."[2] The existence of the universe is explained by assuming two eternal entities;— *Prakṛiti,* described as *amúlam*

[1] "Indian Wisdom," p. 87.
[2] Ib. pp. 97, 98.

mûlam, "a rootless root," and *purusha,* "the soul." All that exists is derived by a process of evolution from *Prakriti,* except *purusha,* which is regarded as apathetic, inactive, and without qualities, though in close connexion with the former: a theory which, very possibly, is connected closely with another, widely accepted in India in more recent times, that a female principle, in conjunction with a male, constitute the joint cause of the world.

But although this dreary atheistic or agnostic system prevailed extensively in India till about the Christian era, and still has its adherents, it was not destined to become the finally accepted philosophy of the Hindoos. In the last-named of the Six Systems, the *Vedânta,* the pantheism, the germs of which had appeared so long ago as the days of the Rig Veda, was developed into a pure monistic pantheism, which is the religious creed of the great majority of the Hindoos at the present day. The whole system is logically involved in one short phrase from the *Chándogya Upanishad:* "*Ekam evâdwitîyam,*" "one only without a second";

a thought which is more fully stated in the line, "*Brahma satyaṃ jagan mithyá jívo brahmaiva náparaḥ.*" "*Brahma* is real, the world is unreal; the soul is very *Brahma*, and no other." Either of these lines one may hear almost any day from the lips of Hindoos in India, as expressing what to their mind is the sum of all philosophic and religious truth. On this pantheistic foundation, has been raised the whole immense structure of modern Puranic Hindooism. On this principle, any and every form of worship that any one may prefer, is readily justified; whether it be the worship of *nature*, as in the adoration of the sun, of *deified men*, as in the most popular worship of *Rám* and of *Krishna*, or that of the *linga* or *phallus*, — in a word, of the grandest and noblest, or of the most insignificant and unworthy, and most revolting objects; as image-worship also, which in the Vedic days was wholly unknown.

It is true that from time to time, — as in the case, *e.g.*, of some of the earlier *Nyáya* teachers, and commentators on the *Sánkhya*, as also in later times, such reformers as *Râmânand, Râmânuja*, and, under the influence of Islâm, *Kabîr* and others, — individuals have sought to break away from absolute bondage to this pantheistic philosophy and regain the primitive faith in one personal God. But, at the best, such individuals have themselves only succeeded in a partial and imperfect degree, and have never been able to draw any great number of the people after them.

These facts as to the order of the development of religion in India are so well known to every one who has studied the subject, and, in particular, have been so fully admitted by Professor Max Müller, that we can only account for his assertion that the movement of Indian thought has been through polytheism to monotheism, by the supposition that he uses the word "monotheism" in a sense peculiar to himself. Monotheism, in the common sense of that word, is repudiated by the Hindoos, almost with one consent. Their own mind on the matter is well expressed by the following words, which are taken from an able antichristian tract, recently issued by a Hindoo Tract Society in North India: —

"Every religion in the world has its own excrescences and its incrustations. We have had our own share of them. But amid all our wanderings and errors we have never degraded ourselves so far as to believe in a personal God . . . to such an extent as to make such a belief a necessary article of faith."[1]

We have dwelt at considerable length upon the historic development of the Indo-Aryan religion, not only because the facts are so thoroughly ascertained, but because it has been so positively asserted, and by so high authority, that the tendency of the religious thought of India has been steadily toward monotheism; an assertion which, we repeat, can only be justified by assuming for the term "monotheism" a meaning which, however consistent with its etymology, in actual use it never has. If monotheism be the truth, then

[1] Quoted in "The Indian Standard," Sept. 1, 1891; in the article "A Remarkable Antichristian Tract."

the history of Indian thought has been marked, not by progress, but by regress; by an invincible tendency away from monotheism, through nature-worship, to pantheism.

The greatest thinkers of India through the by-gone centuries, have not been gradually approaching the conception of God as one and personal, but have steadily drifted away from it. In the pre-Vedic period and in the earliest beginning of the Vedic age, the Indo-Aryans seem to have still retained a conception, somewhat hazy and ill-defined, of one Father in heaven; and even when worshipping God under the forms and names of natural objects and visible phenomena, they recognised Him as one, and as a personal Power. everywhere manifest behind the visible and material world. But now and for centuries past, the people of India, as a whole, with one consent have identified the Creator with the creature, the Most Holy One with the sinner, and therewith continually justify themselves, not only for every form of polytheism, fetish-worship, idol-worship, or no worship at all, but no less, by a logic which on their premises is unanswerable, for the commission of the grossest impurities and the most flagrant crimes.

If we have justly inferred from the intimations in the earliest Vedic hymns, and earlier pre-Vedic period, that the monotheism which was already then disappearing, was the recognised faith of the people of Iran, we should naturally expect to find some further testimony to this fact in the closely related Zend-speaking people of ancient Persia, from the midst of whom, in pre-historic times, the Indo-Aryans emigrated south-eastward into India.

And this expectation is not disappointed. According to Professor Max Müller, the religion of Zoroaster, still professed by the modern Parsees, was originally "founded on a solemn protest against the worship of nature involved in the Vedas."[1]

It is indeed true that in the form which is most familiar, the form in which the Zoroastrian religion maintained itself for centuries,

---

[1] But this is strenuously denied by Darmesteter. See "The Vendidad," Introduction, pp. lxxix, lxxxi ; "Sacred Books of the East," vol. iv.

not monotheism, but dualism, with an idolatrous reverence for the elements, and especially for fire, has been its most characteristic feature. But in the earliest authorities on the Zoroastrian religion this dualism is not yet developed. According to Darmesteter, there is no evidence that this dualism was generally accepted by the ancient Persians before the end of the Achamænian dynasty, about 331 B.C.[1] There is indeed evidence that, before this, the so-called Magi held this dualistic faith, but it had not gained general acceptance.[2] Furthermore, in the *Gáthas*, which form the most ancient portion of the Zendavesta, the idea of two creators, one good, the other evil, is expressly excluded: and *Ahuramazda* is declared to have created all things, the evil as well as the good; as in the following passage : — [3]

[1] "Sacred Books of the East," vol. iv., pp. xliii, xliv.
[2] Ib. pp. xlv, xlvi.
[3] Yasna, xliv, 5 *et seq.* of the Zendavesta. The translation presented is given in an essay by R. Brown, F.S.A., on "The Religion of Zoroaster," read before the Victoria Institute. A more literal translation, essentially identical, will be found in the "Sacred Books of the East," vol. xxxi.

"That I shall ask thee, tell it me right, O *Ahura!*
 Who was in the beginning the father and creator of
    righteousness?
 Who created the path of the sun and stars?
 Who causes the moon to increase and wane, but thou?
 Who is holding the earth and the skies above it?
 Who made the waters and the trees of the field?
 Who created the lights, of good effect, and the darkness?
 Who created the sleep of good effect and the activity?
 Who created the morning, noon, and night?
 Who has prepared the Bactrian home?
 To become acquainted with these things, I approach
    thee, O *Mazda,*
 Beneficent Spirit! Creator of *all* beings!
 That I shall ask thee, tell it me right, O *Ahura!*"

Elsewhere *Ahuramazda* is described as "he who created by means of his wisdom the good and the evil mind."

But along with those earliest utterances, we find others which exhibit the germ of that dualism which was afterward so fully developed.

Thus we read in the *Gáthas:* —

"Thus are the primeval spirits, who as a pair (combining their opposite strivings), and (yet each) independent in his action, have been famed (of old). (They are) a better thing, they two, and a worse, as to thought, and word, and as to deed. And between these two let the wisely acting choose aright. (Choose ye) not (as) the evil-doers!"[1]

Zoroaster was a monotheist. But were, then, the Iranians in the days when the *Gáthas* were written still monotheists? Evidently not; for in these same *Gáthas* is constantly denounced the worship of the *devas*, "the priests and the prophets of idols." Already, then, the Iranian branch of the Aryan race had become polytheists and idolaters. But, according to these same most ancient authorities, this polytheism was not original. Zoroaster speaks, as it were, as a prophet, even as Mohammed to the Arabian idolaters in a later day; not announcing a new religion, but calling them back to an earlier and a purer faith which they had forsaken,

[1] Yasna, xxx, 3, "Sacred Books of the East," vol. xxxi, p. 29. On this Yasna, Mr. Mills, the translator, remarks that it is the "earliest statement of dualism which has come down to us." Yet these two heads are called, "not two persons, or at least not only two persons, but a better thing, or principle, and a worse one. (The qualifying words are all in the neuter.) It is also noticeable that the name Angra Mainya does not occur in this section." — Op. cit., p. 25.

the worship of *Ahura*, the "All-Wise Spirit." For the authority with which he summons the people to the worship of this one and living God, he appeals to "sayings of old which *Ahura* revealed."[1]

And yet, while, as we have just seen, Zoroaster, according to the *Gâthas*, professed and taught faith in one God, he used expressions which, howsoever intended by him, contained the germs of a new dualistic degeneration of the primitive faith. The "twin spirits" of *Ahuramazda*, which at first represented only the two sides of the Divine activity, were soon conceived of as two beings, the one, *Ahuramazda*, the other, *Angromainyus*, or *Ahrimàn*,

[1] The above representations are accepted by learned Parsees as correct. Thus, in a Parsee catechism, prepared, consequent upon the modern missionary activity in Bombay, some years ago, the following questions and answers, among others, are given:—

"*Q.* Whom do we of the Zurthosti religion believe in?

"*A.* We believe in one only God, and do not believe in any besides Him.

"*Q.* What religion prevailed in Persia before the time of Zurthost?

"*A.* The kings and the people were worshippers of God; but they had, like the Hindoos, images of the planets and idols in their temples."— See in "Religious Systems of the World," pp. 174, 175.

the Evil One, the Great Serpent. The latter was regarded as independent and self-existent, but as differing from *Ahuramazda*, in that he lacks foresight, so that he will at last be defeated. To these two, again, were added a multitude of inferior beings, personifications, many of them, of the good or evil attributes supposed to belong to *Ahuramazda* or *Angromainyus;* the *Amesha spentas* on the side of the former and an army of demons, *Akemano*, *Taric*, and the rest, on the side of the latter.

Yet in this new dualism and polydemonism the mind could not rest, and in various sects an effort was made to include the two, the good and the evil principle, in a third, from which they both were supposed to proceed; especially in an abstraction, *Zrvan Akarana*, "Boundless Space." But speculations of this kind never seem to have gained general acceptance. If one may accept without qualification the representations of such eminent Parsees as *Dādābhai Nāoroji*, the modern Parsees must indeed in fairness be described as monotheists.[1]

[1] "Religious Systems of the World," v, p. 182.

But none the less does the history of the Zoroastrian religion confirm the general proposition, that man shows, as a law of his religious development, an invincible tendency to degeneration, only arrested or retarded in any successful degree where we are able to trace the influence of that special line of monotheistic thought represented, in the first instance, in the Hebrew Scriptures, and then in the New Testament and the Quran, which represent diverse descendants of the same original stock. It must not be forgotten that the followers of Zoroaster, through most of their history, first in the first Jewish dispersion, then, in later days, through contact with Nestorian Christianity and with Islam, and, last of all, now with modern Christian missionary work, have been almost from the first exposed to influences which should help them to hold on in an exceptional way to the monotheism of the earliest *Gâthas*, and so retard the usual degeneration.

Unlike the religions of Egypt, of India, and of Persia, that of the ancient Babylonians, in the earliest period to which extant records ascend, presents no certain suggestion of a monotheistic faith.[1] The earliest literature which has been deciphered is that of the "Magical Texts." It covers a period extending back for an unknown time prior to the rise of the Shemitic supremacy, about 3750 B.C., in the Euphrates valley, under Sargon I. These texts, so far as published, exhibit among that ancient Turanian people in the lower Euphrates valley nothing higher than a superstitious animism, with its professional exorcists, who claimed to be able, by the use of various spells and incantations, to deliver men from the malign influence of numberless spirits believed to exist in the various objects of nature. Of the idea of a God, in our high sense of the word, in this literature, so far as published, we have found no certain trace.

Among the countless spirits recognised, appear references to the spirits of heaven and

[1] Our chief authority for what is said regarding the Babylonian religion, is Professor Sayce. See The Hibbert Lectures, 1879, "The Origin and Growth of Religion, as illustrated by the Religion of Ancient Egypt."

of the earth, as specially eminent. These seem, then, to have been conceived of separately from the natural objects which they were supposed to animate, and were gradually developed into creative gods. In Southern Babylonia, in this period, about the city of Eridu, on the Persian Gulf, appears the worship of *Ea*, or *Oannes*, the god of culture or of wisdom, and in Northern Babylonia, that of *Mul-lil*, the lord of the ghost world. A god of fire was also specially worshipped, who afterward was identified with the Sun-god.

As this earliest known period approached its close, a little before 3750 B.C., appear the oldest of the so-called "Penitential Psalms," a literature distinguished by a very marked development of the sense of sin, though yet without any very clear expression of monotheistic belief. In these, with the "god, known or unknown," frequently invoked, is associated a goddess, whose pardon and favour also is begged; a circumstance in which, in the opinion of Professor Sayce, we are to recognise the first trace of the rising influence of Shemitic thought upon that of the Turanian race.

ORDER OF RELIGIOUS DEVELOPMENT. 233

The Shemitic political supremacy, which began with Sargon I, introduced a new stage of religious development, in which the earlier animism gradually sank to a subordinate position, and was supplanted by the higher conceptions of the Shemitic nature-worship. In this the Sun-god, variously known in his various aspects as *Samas*, or *Merodach*, or *Adar*, appears as the head of a divine family, in which he stands forth as omnipotent creator. With him are associated a goddess, — after the usual Shemitic fashion, — as also the Moon-god, and a host of minor deities, which at a later day are said to be no less than forty-five thousand in number. And this type of religion continued to prevail in the Euphrates valley region until the final downfall of the Babylonian power, in the sixth century B.C.

Such, then, was the order of the development of religion among the Babylonians. Earliest of all, we find a worship of spirits, with which natural objects were supposed to be animated; then gradually, under external Shemitic influence, arose a system of nature-worship, especially that of the sun, the moon, and the stars, conceived of later in an anthropomorphic way, and each associated with a female counterpart, or goddess.

Connected with this religious development we find, as in India and elsewhere, that a religious philosophy gradually arose. The god *Ana* (Shem. *Anu*), originally the god of the visible sky, became first the "supreme lord of the universe," the "one god against whom none may rebel." But this supreme god of that time was only conceived of in a pantheistic manner, and was identified with the universe itself. On the other hand, while some resolved all that exists into the Divine, last of all, others maintained that matter itself was the one substance and primal cause of all that is, even of the great gods themselves. In either case alike, the tendency was, not to monotheism, but to monism.

Now it is indeed true that extant sources, so far as yet known, have not hitherto revealed, in the distant antiquity of the Akkadian supremacy in the Euphrates valley, any distinct recognition of God as one, living, and personal; and thus they afford us no direct evidence of a degeneration of religion from this higher conception to the ancient Akkadian animism. But it is of the first importance to observe that throughout the whole four thousand years or more of Babylonian history, there is no indication whatever of any tendency to the evolution of a monotheistic faith. Instead of this, we find a polytheism which, if higher in an intellectual aspect than the animism which preceded it, yet ever exhibits more and more of awful moral degradation; and along with this, as in other lands, here pantheism, and there materialism, both alike excluding the idea of a God, one and personal, as the Creator and Governor of the world.

Hence, the facts, when thoughtfully considered, give no support for the opinion which one might hastily form, that Babylonian history, at least, must be allowed to sustain the theory of the development of monotheism out of a primitive animism. It is true that the early animism of the early Akkadians was succeeded by forms of religion which, regarded merely from an intellectual point of view, were less degraded than the religion of the Magical Texts. But even this improvement, of such sort as it was, cannot be ascribed to any native tendency to develop a higher form of religion among those Turanian peoples, but only, as Sayce and Lenormant have shown, to the influence of Shemitic thought. But even when this became dominant, the movement of religious thought was still not toward monotheism, but rather, as in Egypt and India, toward an increasing polytheism, justified or excused by a pantheistic or a materialistic philosophy.

If, then, the tendency of Babylonian thought, throughout the whole historic period, was indisputably in another direction than towards monotheism, it is obviously most illogical and unscientific to assume that in the prehistoric period the tendency had been the reverse. And thus we are led to recognise in the early animism of the Euphrates valley Akkadians, nothing primitive, but rather an extreme degeneration of religion from an earlier and purer form, such as history compels us to recognise in the case of other peoples, where the historic process can be more clearly traced.

About 2200 B.C., the date when trustworthy history begins in China, according to Dr. Legge and other high authorities,[1] the Chinese were, as now, worshipping the heaven and the earth, and the spirits of their ancestors. By the name "Heaven," however, he understands that they really, in the first instance, denoted the Supreme God. That it *might* have been so, we shall easily see when we remember that even among ourselves the word "Heaven" is often used for the Supreme Being; and that in this we have the warrant, as he reminds us, even of the New Testament; as in Luke xv, where the prodigal son is made to say: "I have sinned against Heaven." Besides the worship of heaven, the Chinese worshipped other objects in nature, as the earth, the sun, moon, and stars, and also the spirits of their ancestors; all of which cults have survived to the present time.

But against the opinion of some, that nature-worship was the earliest form of religion among the Chinese, Dr. Legge adduces the

[1] "Religious Systems of the World," London, 1890, pp. 46, 47.

pertinent testimony of Confucius, that by the ceremonies of the sacrifices to heaven and earth "they worship God." So in prayers addressed to the "Rain Master," the "Cloud Master," and others, these are declared to be "ministers assisting the Supreme God."[1] Such expressions as these seem indeed to imply that in early times, as in India the worshippers of Varuna, so the Chinese had still a lingering consciousness of the unity and personality of God. But, if one may trust the testimony of missionaries and others who have long lived among the people, the official worship of heaven and earth by the emperor, in modern times, is now, and for a long time past has been, an unqualified idolatry. Such assure us that heaven, as thus worshipped, is not now regarded as a term for God: it denotes the visible heaven deified. That the primitive ancestors of the Chinese may have at first worshipped the one God under the name and symbol of the over-arching heaven, if we may reason from the analogy of religious history among other peoples, is likely enough; but

[1] "Religious Systems of the World," p. 48.

for centuries the idea of God has practically disappeared from the consciousness of the whole Chinese nation. It has been utterly lost in a worship of nature, of spirits numberless, of idols, and of the departed dead. As regards this most popular ancestor-worship, Dr. Legge indeed insists that even the spirit of Confucius himself receives merely the worship of gratitude for his great services to the nation, and not the worship of adoration, such as is proper to God alone.[1] However, granting that this may have been so in the beginning, even Dr. Legge speaks of the danger that this worship may lead to superstition and idolatry, and gives an example of this in the actual deification of Kwan Yu, a famous warrior of the third Christian century, who has become to the Chinese the god of war.[2] Missionaries, with one accord, assure us that this danger has long ago been universally realised in fact.

Whatever may have been the monotheism of the primitive days of the Chinese nation, nothing is more certain than that, at the very

[1] "Religious Systems of the World," p. 51.   [2] Ib. p. 52.

beginning of the historic period, it had become, practically, an inoperative belief, if indeed held at all. In later days, as is well known, Confucius carefully avoided teaching anything as to the Supreme Being, or the relations of man to heaven. It was enough that the emperor offered sacrifices at the proper time to the spirits of heaven and of earth. If man had any relations to God, any duties owed to Heaven, Confucius ignored them. Professor Beal tells us that, throughout the whole period of more than two thousand years down to about 209 B.C., while there had been much of material and of intellectual activity among the Chinese, there was " never a sign of any spiritual life or aspiration."[1] Lao Tze had in the mean time appeared, but neither did he, any more than Confucius, speak a word concerning the living and true God. The *Tao* of which he had so much to say, whatever may have been intended by the word, was not "God." That *Tao* denoted any personal being is expressly denied.[2] And,

[1] " Religious Systems of the World," p. 74.
[2] Thus, e.g., Chuang Tzu says: " *Tao* is impersonal and passionless." Ib. p. 57. See also pp. 59, 60.

though the writings of the "Old Philosopher," and some few of his disciples, contain some sentiments which are admirable in their moral character, yet Taoism, destitute of moral power, has degenerated until all agree that it represents little else to-day than a confused agglomeration of superstitious beliefs in evil spirits, and various magical arts for their exorcism. Practically, this most ancient of all existing nations gives one of the most impressive proofs to be found in all history, that in humanity is no innate tendency toward monotheism, but rather a most persistent and inveterate inclination away from the very thought of God, to the most debased and superstitious forms of religion.

In the whole four thousand years covered by authentic Chinese history, we thus search in vain for any evidence of a tendency to advance toward higher and purer conceptions of divine things. If Dr. Legge is right in his belief, that, according to the Chinese authorities, monotheism was really recognised in the earliest times, then it is certain that from that faith they have utterly fallen away. If the ancestor-worship was not at first, as Dr. Legge thinks, idolatrous in character, it seems, without doubt, to have long ago become so. If, on the other hand, as many of the best scholars in China think, Dr. Legge is mistaken in the interpretation of the Chinese classics, by which he sustains his contention for their original monotheism, it is still certain that, during the whole period of trustworthy Chinese history, that people have shown not the slightest tendency to develop a monotheistic religion, but, on the contrary, like other races, a constant inclination to religious debasement.

Such, then, are the facts with regard to the peoples of culture. We find among them, with the single exception of the Shemitic people of Israel, no instance either of a nation which has retained an original monotheism, or which has gradually risen from some lower faith to a monotheistic religion. If this be true of the nations of culture, it is no less true of barbarous tribes. In a multitude of instances, the traditions of such degraded peoples remarkably confirm the testimony of cultivated races to an original faith in one God, living and true, the great God above all gods. Of this fact, only a few illustrations can be given. Among the aboriginal tribes of India, the most numerous and important are the Santâls. These are at present worshippers of demons, an extremely degraded people, without an alphabet, and without a literature. Their worship chiefly consists in various rites intended to propitiate a multitude of evil spirits, with whom they suppose themselves to be surrounded. But their tradition, already referred to,[1] witnesses that it was not always so. They say that at first they worshipped the one God, who in the beginning made one man and one woman; that the Evil Spirit, *Marang Buru*, appearing to their first parents under the form of a great mountain, persuaded them to make a drink of the fruit of a certain tree, by which they became intoxicated. Because of this, God was angry, and they came under the power of *Marang Buru* and the other evil spirits under him, to whom, therefore, they

[1] Sup. p. 61.

must now present their offerings, instead of to God.

The closely related Kolhs have in like manner retained the memory of a primitive faith in one invisible God, whom they call *Sing Bongà*, who created all things. But he is regarded as practically far away, and their worship is chiefly rendered, like that of the Santals, to a multitude of evil spirits.

On the other side of the world, the ancient Peruvians, and the still more ancient and aboriginal *Aimares*, had preserved the tradition of a primitive monotheistic faith. They had this quaint tradition. Because God was all alone, he longed for some one to love him. And so he made *Kuru*, the first man. And *Kuru* had a son, and the son died. And God said unto *Kuru*: "Thy son shall rise again from the dead; eat not therefore of the fruit which grows from his grave." But *Kuru* disobeyed this command of God. And God said unto him: "Because thou hast not obeyed me, thou shalt have toil, and thou shalt die; and all men shall die with thee."

The fetish-worshipping negroes of the West Coast of Africa, in like manner, confess as primitive, a faith in one invisible God, the Creator and Ruler of all, who at first held communion with their fathers, as he does now no longer. They call him *Kopong*, or *Onjang Kopong*, a word apparently identical with the word *Kubong*, for " God," used by the aborigines of Australia, and the word *Bonga*, " God," among the Kolh aborigines of India. Indeed, the full name, *Onjang Kopong*, has the very same meaning with the phrase *Sing Bonga*, " Shining Spirit," which the Kolhs use to denote the Supreme Being.

As all know, many traditions and religious usages of the American Indians tell, in like manner, of a Great Spirit, who is above all, sometimes, indeed, confounded with heroes of olden times, but often, again, distinctly referred to as the invisible Being who has made all that is. Thus, the Chippewas pray to *Manedo*, called by the Delawares *Manitowa Manitou*, who, they say, is the Creator of the world. Besides him, we are told, they worship neither sun, nor moon, nor any god. To multiply examples is needless.

With the single exception, then, of the Shemitic people of Israel, there is no instance of any of the peoples of antiquity, whether cultured or uncultured, gradually rising from the worship of nature, of fetishes, or of ancestors, to that of the one living and true God. Where among any ancient people we find indications of monotheistic belief, these are most conspicuous, not in the latest, but in the earliest period of their history. The history of religion exhibits, as a general law, a tendency to fall away from the purity of monotheistic faith, wherever in an earlier time it has been held. Hence, the hypothesis that man began his religious life with some low form of religion, from which, by a normal process of natural development, monotheism has been at last evolved, is not sustained by facts. These point to a conclusion which is the exact reverse of this; a conclusion which, however irreconcilable with modern theories of evolution, is in perfect harmony with the presumption already established by the consideration of the potency of sin as an omnipresent factor in the development of religion. The only inference which is justified by the facts thus far reviewed is this: that man began with the knowledge — very elementary, no doubt, but, none the less, correct — of God, his Creator, as a Being, one and personal like himself; and that animism, polytheism, pantheism, atheism, and all other forms of religion or religious philosophy, must be regarded as various forms of degeneration from that primitive faith.

LECTURE VIII.

SHEMITIC MONOTHEISM. — CONCLUSION.

In the previous lecture it has been shown that in the Indo-Germanic and Turanian races there is no evidence of a general tendency to the evolution of a monotheistic faith, but rather the reverse. In those cases where monotheistic conceptions have found expression in the literature of a people, as in Egypt, India, and Persia, these have been chiefly characteristic, not of the latest, but of the earliest, stage of their religious development. The tendency throughout the whole historic period, in every such case, has been to fall away from monotheism into nature-worship of various forms, ancestor-worship, polytheism, fetishism, and idolatry. And if among the educated classes the idea of the unity of the First Cause of the universe has been attained or preserved, it has commonly been under the perverted forms of pantheism or materialism, in which τὸ μόνον has been substituted for ὁ μόνος, an impersonal substance, acting under the laws of necessity, in the place of a personal God, working in nature and in providence as an almighty free agent.

In other instances, again, the earliest records of a people, as, *e.g.*, those of the Akkadians of the Euphrates valley, and perhaps the Chinese, disclose no certain evidence of the existence, in the most ancient period of their history, of a monotheistic belief, but, instead, either a worship of ancestors, as among the latter, or of various elemental spirits, as among the former. Still, it has appeared that such cases in reality give no support to the theory of a naturalistic evolution of a monotheistic religion: for the reason that, throughout their whole history, extending, in the case of the peoples mentioned, over thousands of years, no tendency, however slight, has been manifest, toward the development of a monotheistic belief, but, instead, a progressive lapse into forms of religion ever more and more debased and corrupt.

Hence, inasmuch as, in the absence of evidence to the contrary, it must be supposed that the law of religious tendency must have been the same in prehistoric times as since, we have therefore been led to conclude that the supposition that man must have begun with some extremely low and superstitious type of religion, from which, by slow degrees, in a purely natural way, under an eternal law of progress, he has advanced, at last, in many instances at least, to the faith in one personal God, must be rejected as irreconcilable with such facts as have been presented. If we may legitimately infer the unknown past from the past which is known, the inference seems unavoidable that not animism, or fetishism, or some vague type of nature-worship, but a simple form of monotheism, must have been the primitive faith of man, of which all other forms of religion exhibit various degrees of degeneration and debasement.

But it has been maintained that to this general law as to the order of the development of religion, at least one exception must be admitted, so important as to nullify the force of the above argument. It is said that in the Shemitic race, at least, we have an undeniable example of the gradual evolution of a monotheistic faith from an original low type of religion; so that the assertion of a *universal* law to the contrary is thereby disproved. For, it is argued, since a natural evolution of monotheism has certainly taken place in this great division of the human race, within historic times, it is quite possible that such a law of development may have prevailed universally in prehistoric times; so that there is nothing to forbid our supposing that the religious life of man may have begun with some very low form of belief, from which he gradually rose until he attained such sublime conceptions of the Supreme Being as are expressed, for example, in the most ancient religion of Egypt.

By such writers it is often claimed that this has been, indeed, the special glory of the Shemitic race, as contrasted with others; that it has been endowed with a peculiar genius for religion. This is said to have been its distinguishing characteristic, as truly as a genius for art was that of the ancient Greeks, and a genius for law and government was that of the ancient Romans. Renan, among others, has affirmed this, with characteristic assurance, as one of the great race contrasts, in such words as the following: —

"The Indo-European race, distracted by the variety of the universe, never by itself arrived at monotheism. The Shemitic race, on the contrary, guided by its firm and sure sight, instantly unmasked Divinity, and without reflection or reasoning attained the purest form of religion that humanity has known."[1]

Again: —

"When and how did the Shemitic race arrive at this notion of the divine unity, which the world has admitted on the faith of its teaching? I think it was by a primitive intuition, and from its earliest days. . . . The Shemitic race . . . reached, evidently

---

[1] "Studies of Religious History and Criticism," authorised translation, Amer. ed., p. 115.

without an effort, the notion of the Supreme God."[1]

These are fine words, but is the assertion true? Is the Shemitic monotheism rightly explained as a mere natural product of an exceptional race genius? This is the question to which we address ourselves in the present lecture. Or, as it has been felicitously put by Professor Ebrard: "Is the one God a product of Israel, or is Israel a product of the one God?"[2]

We at once admit the Shemitic monotheism as a fact. And the fact is the more significant, when we call to mind that only as preached, in the first instance, by Shemitic prophets and apostles, has monotheism ever become to any extent a victorious power over heathenism and heathen philosophy. Among non-Shemitic peoples monotheism has only successfully maintained a supremacy in so far as these have come more or less directly under the influence of Shemitic thought, as

[1] "Studies of Religious History and Criticism," authorised translation, Amer. ed., pp. 115, 116. [2] "Apologetik," 2 Bd. § 306.

expressed either in Judaism, Christianity, or Islam. The monotheism of ancient Egypt, of the primitive Aryans in India and Persia, as we have seen, was unable to maintain itself successfully against the inborn tendency of man to debase the ideal of religious faith. Shemitic monotheism alone has shown itself a conquering and transforming power in the history of the world.

Again, whether or not we attribute to the Shemitic races a special religious genius, of which their monotheism is the product, it is to be admitted that among them, as Principal Fairbairn has well shown, a higher conception of the Divine nature seems to have originally prevailed than among the Indo-Germanic races. This is conclusively shown by a comparison of the oldest names used in each race to designate the Deity. While these names among the Indo-Germanic races were commonly derived from the forces and phenomena of material nature, the earliest and most universal names of God among the Shemitic peoples designate the Deity instead by moral and metaphysical attributes, rightly imputed to the Supreme Being.

As a familiar example of the former may be taken the Sanskrit word *deva*, from the root *div*, "to shine," thus literally meaning "the shining one," whence have come the Latin *deus*, the Old German *Tio*, etc., etc., to which may be added the other Vedic name of deity, *dyaus*, "the heaven," which appears also in the Greek *Zeus*, and the first syllable of the Latin *Ju-piter*.

In contrast with a large number of names of this character may be noted the old Assyrian *Ilu*, Heb. *El*, from a root meaning "to be strong," thus denoting the Deity as "the Mighty One"; *Eloah*, plur. *Elohim*, Ar. *Allâh*, from a root signifying "to tremble," and so "to fear," thus denoting God as the proper object of fear and of worship. So, in the Hebrew Scriptures we meet with such compound appellatives as *El Elyon*, "God the Most High," a term which has also been found in a letter sent to Egypt from a priest-king reigning in Jerusalem, — after the manner of

Melchizedek at an earlier day, — about one hundred and fifty years before Moses. Again, we have *El Shaddai*, designating God as the "All-bountiful One," the great Giver of all, and *Yahveh*, "He who is," or "who will be," the Self-existent One. Marked by the same characteristic are the names common in the Shemitic heathenism, such as *Ba'al*, "Owner," "Lord"; *Molech*, "King"; *Adonis*, "the Lord," etc., etc.

This general statement of the common failure of the non-Shemitic races to attain such conceptions of the Deity as the Shemitic terms for God express, must be qualified by at least two or three conspicuous exceptions. Of these, the chief are the old Egyptian *Nutar*, as a name of Deity, meaning, precisely, "the Power," never used in the plural number,[1] and *Nuk pu nuk*, nearly equivalent to the Hebrew *Yahveh*; and the old Magian word, *Ahuramazda*, "the All-knowing Spirit." Still in none of these cases did such conceptions ever obtain that exclusive dominance in religion as in the case of the Shemitic races.

[1] See Renouf: "Origin and Growth of Religion," pp. 98–100.

Of these Shemitic names for God, such as are common to all the Shemitic peoples point back distinctly to a time when they had not yet become scattered, and in their primitive home together held that high conception of *El*, or *Ilu*, God, as "the Mighty One," or *Elohim*, the Supreme Object of fear and worship. In these most ancient names of God there is nothing to suggest that they at first denoted some dead ancestor, or a ghost, or some object in physical nature. They indicate a primitive monotheism, and that of a high ethical type.

But was this Shemitic monotheism due merely to a natural and ineffaceable race-characteristic, in virtue of which they alone, so early in their history, found their way up quickly from a worship of nature, of ghosts or fetishes, to the exalted conception of *El Elyon?* If so, then we should expect to find evidence of this tendency in the historic records of the race. Of this, however, there is no evidence, but, instead, of the contrary. Among all of the Shemitic peoples alike, history bears witness to the operation of the same invincible tendency to religious degradation which we have seen to exist in the other great branches of the human family.

As regards the early Shemites of the Euphrates valley, when they first come before us, in the reign of Sargon I, 3750 B.C., they are already polytheists, and throughout the whole thirty-one hundred years of Assyrian history, from Sargon I to the time when Shemitic empire finally went down under Cyrus the Great, there is not the slightest evidence of any tendency to monotheism. Notwithstanding the many high-sounding names of God on the lips of the people, bearing silent witness to the pure faith of an unrecorded antiquity, these Euphrates Shemites not only showed the same tendency to religious degeneration as their Indo-Germanic and Turanian neighbours, but they exhibited this in a peculiarly aggravated form. Already, when in prehistoric times the clans who peopled Arabia left the Shemitic race-centre in the Euphrates valley, they appear to have carried with them that worship of the heavenly bodies which we find prevailing when authentic Assyrian history opens with Sargon I. As for the section of the race which was left behind, it was their evil pre-eminence over their Akkadian neighbours that in their conception of God they emphasised the idea of generation over that of creation, and first introduced into the conception of the Deity the idea of sexual distinction. And this, again, became, as all know, the most prolific source of those unutterable abominations perpetrated in the name of religion, because of which, in later days, when the deadly evil had reached Canaan, God, according to the Hebrew Scriptures, not without just reason, commanded the Canaanites to be extirpated from the earth.

Thus it was precisely these ancient Shemites, whose religious genius, and sublime intuition of the one God, Renan calls upon us to admire, who debased the conception of God to a degree which, so far as we know, had never been reached before, and even since has been never exceeded. It was their infamous distinction that in their idolatrous madness they, first, declared the most atrocious cruelties and the most horrible and unnatural lusts to be precisely that kind of service with which Deity was specially pleased. It is certainly with abundant reason that Ebrard describes this old Shemitic religion as "a demoniac, Satanic crime against the innate moral law, and therewith a fundamental destruction of conscience, and perversion of the knowledge of God;"[1] or, more vividly still, speaking of its Phœnician development, as a "wilful repetition of the primeval fall, — a fall from a condition of simple sinfulness into a diabolic, demoniac obduracy, — an infamous revolt against God, and against conscience."[2] And out of the indescribable depths of that polytheistic nature-worship into which the Euphrates Shemites so early sank, they never arose. Among them we search in vain for any trace of the alleged Shemitic tendency to a pure monotheistic religion.

With the Arabian Shemites, although, so far as we know, they never descended to such an abyss of religious debasement as those whom

[1] "Apologetik," 2 Bd. § 173.   [2] Ib. § 177.

they left behind in the Euphrates valley, the case, as regards our argument, was not essentially different. Above the worship of nature to which they early gave themselves, through four thousand years or more, they never rose. Then, indeed, Muhammed appeared, preaching among them the almost forgotten truths of the unity and personality of God, and the Arabians followed him. But the monotheism of Muhammed, so far as one can judge from the Quran and the *Ahádís*, must be ascribed in a great degree to Jewish and Christian influence. Nor was even he able wholly to eradicate the venerable system of idolatry which opposed him; but, as in the case of the famous black stone, the Kaaba at Mecca, he was constrained to allow something to remain as a necessary concession to the ancient Shemitic heathenism.

Elsewhere than among the Arabian Shemites shall we then have to look, for that monotheistic tendency for which we seek. We turn last of all to the Hebrew race. Here, at least, it is insisted, we shall find one brilliant illustration of that natural evolution of monotheistic re-

ligion from a lower form of faith, for which
we have thus far sought in vain. But what
are the facts? Is there historical evidence
to prove that the Hebrews were distinguished
from other branches of the Shemitic race by
a natural tendency to monotheism, which is
the sufficient explanation of all that is most
distinctive in their religious history? For the
answer to this question, we must inquire of the
Hebrew Scriptures. We appeal to them, in
this instance, not as inspired, but simply as
presenting a historical record of the Hebrew
nation from the days before Abraham to the
end of the Babylonian captivity. In estimating
the value of this testimony, it is safe to assume,
on the principles which govern human nature,
that the writers of the several books of the
Old Testament are not likely to have given
us an unduly unfavourable picture of the
religious history of their nation. If a large
part of these records were written so very late
as the modern radical criticism supposes, at
a time when, after the Babylonian captivity,
the nation as a whole had become emancipated

from polytheism and idolatry, all the more we should be led to anticipate that, through a spirit of national pride, they would rather be inclined to represent the religious history of the nation in as favourable light as possible.

In view of this consideration, all the more significant it appears that the Jewish historians, with one accord, should have represented the religious history of their nation in very dark colours. Most extraordinary, in the light of the facts, is the explanation which Renan gives of the monotheism imputed to Adam and Eve, that with the Israelites monotheism was "such an incontestable truth" that, when describing primitive men, they "could only imagine them monotheists"! Instead of finding it so difficult thus to think of their ancestors, they unanimously represent the history of their nation and of the family from which it sprang, as from before the days of Abraham, marked by an almost invincible tendency to lapse into the most horrible and debasing forms of polytheism and idolatry. In this respect, they were no whit better than their heathen neighbours.

While their records represent Noah, the first ancestor of the post-diluvian peoples, as a believer in *Elohim*, the one living God, we are expressly told that by the time of Terah, 2200 B.C., and we know not how long before, the ancestors of the Israelitish nation were worshippers of other gods.[1] There can be little doubt that Abraham himself, living as he did, in Ur of the Chaldees, at that time the chief seat of the worship of Sin, the moon-god, was brought up by his father Terah as a worshipper of the moon. Nor does the record attribute the change which came over Abraham to his religious genius, but to one and another manifestation of that *Ilu*, known indeed by name to his Shemitic neighbours, but worshipped in that day, so far as we know, by none around him. Called in some mysterious way by God to leave the idolatrous surroundings of his early life, we are told that he went down, under Divine guidance, into Canaan, where the iniquity of the Amorites was "not yet full," and where still, at least in the case of Melchizedek, the

[1] Josh. xxiv, 2.

worship of *El Elyon*, the Most High God, apparently had still here and there an adherent; and there made his home until his death.

But if monotheism, under the extraordinary influence of this patriarch, continued in the line of his immediate posterity until, when Joseph was the prime minister of Pharaoh, they went down into Egypt, yet their records state that their descendants, instead of advancing to the more perfect knowledge of God, lapsed readily into the idolatry of their heathen neighbours; — a fact which is attested by their ready acceptance of the worship of the golden calf, set up almost as soon as they left Egypt, at Mount Sinai, in imitation of the Egyptian *Apis*-worship. Nor did the remarkable events of the Exodus under their great monotheistic leader, hinder the Hebrews from persisting in the practice of their polytheistic idolatry until that whole generation had perished in the wilderness.

Nor did the "monotheistic genius" yet show itself when they arrived in Canaan. Commanded to exterminate the idolatrous tribes whose iniquities had then come to the full, and under no circumstances to contract alliances with them, we learn from the books of Joshua and Judges that they not only did not obey this command, but through the days of the judges they found the surrounding heathenism so congenial and attractive, that they again and again forsook the worship of the one living God for that of Baal, Molech, and Ashtoreth.

Under the kings, the same inveterate inclination to idolatry continued to assert itself. If, under David, monotheism reached a temporary ascendency, yet, by the end of Solomon's reign, a new decline from the worship of the one God began to appear; and in the reign of his son Rehoboam, with the secession of the ten tribes under Jeroboam, the old calf-worship was formally established as the religion of the new state. From that time onward to the catastrophe under Hoshea, the history of that part of the Hebrew nation presents one unvarying record of an abandonment, ever more and more complete, of the worship of the only God for the cruel and licentious worship of Baal and Ashtoreth, and other of the old Shemitic naturegods.

Nor did Judah as a people prove an exception to this law of religious degeneration. If now and then monotheistic kings, supported by fearless prophets, sought to bring the people back to the sole worship of *Yahveh*, their success was only temporary, and, as Jeremiah charges, unreal and superficial while it lasted. And so, finally, as in 721 B.C. the kingdom of the ten tribes had gone down under Shalmaneser of Assyria, in 588 B.C. that of Judah also fell, under Nebuchadnezzar of Babylon.

Now it is submitted that this record of more than fifteen hundred years of Hebrew history, is a conclusive refutation of the supposition that the monotheism which at last asserted itself in Israel can be rightly attributed to a racial tendency, in that direction. The whole history, from the days of Terah and Abraham, bears unvarying testimony to the fact that, as with other branches of the Shemitic race, so with Israel, the race tendency was not toward monotheism, but toward a polytheistic nature-worship, and that of an exceptionally horrible and revolting kind.

We may, therefore, without hesitation, affirm that not only is it not true that the Shemitic people, as a whole, have exhibited a peculiar monotheistic genius, and have thus been an exception to the world-wide tendency to fall away from the knowledge and worship of the one living God, but the fact is the reverse. It is just the Shemitic race who have furnished, perhaps, one of the most appalling illustrations of this law of human nature which is known to history. The facts of their history bear testimony to a *special* race proclivity to the grossest and most debasing forms of idolatry, which appears only the more impressive and significant when we recall the fact that, as their primitive names for God reveal, they seem at first to have had a conception of the Deity so much higher than that which is revealed by such names among most other ancient peoples.

Of the non-Shemitic races, some, indeed, never fell so utterly away from the truth concerning God as did, especially, those Shemitic inhabitants of the Euphrates valley; others, indeed, at last reached the same depths of religious debasement; as is witnessed in the incredibly revolting ceremonial of the *Aswamedha*, or horse-sacrifice of ancient India, as prescribed in the Yajur Veda, chap. xxiii, Mantra 18, about the third century B.C., or in the unutterable abominations of the goat-worship practised at Mendes in Upper Egypt. But these all reached these uttermost abysses of religious corruption more slowly. It was the peculiarity of the religious development of the Shemites, whose religious genius Renan so extols, that, from a height in the beginning so much above other nations, they more swiftly than any others descended to a debasement of the idea of God and of his worship, such as many other races never reached, and below which, probably, no race has ever yet sunk. No one who is familiar with the facts will wonder at the remark of Professor Ebrard, that "sin in its highest potency is Shemitic corruption."

The conclusion from this is evident. An adequate cause of the development of the Hebrew monotheism cannot be found in the Hebrew national genius, but only, as the Hebrew records continually assert, in the *supernatural* in-working, in individuals of that selected nation, of the Spirit of the one living and true God. It is not the peculiar glory of Israel, more than of any other people, that by their own exceptional national genius, they arrived at the conception of the one personal God, and gave it to the world. Rather is it the glory of the one God, that, notwithstanding the Shemitic-Hebrew tendency to the grossest polytheism and idolatry,—a tendency even stronger among them than among the Indo-Germanic races,—He yet, through repeated chastisements and undeserved deliverances, and especially by raising up and endowing with supernatural gifts a succession of witnesses for Himself in the midst of a corrupt nation, brought Israel, despite itself, to show forth His praise, and become, in a sense solitary and unique in history, a witness for Himself, that He, *Elohim*, and Jehovah, the *Elohim* of Israel, was God and none else beside Him.

And, finally, if we look at this argument in the light of the history of Israel and of the church from the return from Babylon to the present time, we shall find that it appears all the more conclusive. For — not to speak of the prophets — it is quite impossible to account for Jesus of Nazareth, in the light of this history, as the consummate product of religious evolution in Israel. But into this most important line of argument our limits forbid us to enter. We must content ourselves with affirming that the exception to the general law of religious degeneration from monotheistic faith, which has been asserted in the case of the Shemitic race, and especially of the Hebrew nation, is not established by the facts of history.

We must, therefore, regard the fact as practically universal, that mankind, for whatsoever reason, exhibit a native inclination, more or less pronounced in all races and all ages, to fall away from monotheism, wherever it has existed; on the theoretic side of religion, inclining to pantheism or materialism; on the practical side, into creature-worship, self-worship, and various forms of polytheism and idolatry. The operation of this innate tendency in man has now and then, indeed, been interrupted or retarded, through the influence of commanding personalities, proclaiming anew the fundamental truths of religion; such as Zoroaster, Moses, Isaiah, or, in modern times, a Huss or a Luther. But all the labours of such witnesses for God, have never been able to eradicate this tendency away from Him. Even Christianity has not been exempt from this law of religious degradation, but in most lands has illustrated the same ancient and invincible inclination of mankind to the debasement of the idea of God, and the worship of the creature more than the Creator.

Finally, we affirm that the fact of this tendency, universally exhibited throughout historic times, is utterly irreconcilable with any supposition but that monotheism was the original faith of man; and that all other forms of religion and philosophy only exhibit various lines of declension from the purity of the primitive faith. For to assert the opposite hypothesis.

and make monotheism the goal of the development, involves the unwarranted assumption that the law of the order of religious development in prehistoric times, was the reverse of that which has prevailed everywhere throughout the whole historic period. The assumption takes for granted the existence of a native tendency in man to religious elevation, while the testimony of history exhibits the opposite tendency as a fact practically universal. Such an assumption condemns in advance every theory of the origin and growth of religion which is based upon it.

We venture, therefore, notwithstanding the many names of high repute which may be cited on the other side of this question, to believe that on scientific grounds one can fully justify the biblical representations of the monotheism of the first men, and of the origin of all heathenism, in the natural aversion of all sinful men from God; because of which they did not like to retain Him in their knowledge, and therefore worshipped and served the creature more than the Creator, who is "God over all, blessed forever."

And, last of all, in the light of history, we must add that the great, unique phenomenon of the Hebrew monotheism, as a conquering power through the ages, is inexplicable and unaccountable on merely natural grounds. No adequate cause for it can be found in Shemitic nature or in Hebrew genius. It only receives a satisfying explanation when it is recognised as due, even as the Holy Scriptures continually assert, to the supernatural grace and special providence of the one living God, working redemptively in history through chosen individuals of a chosen race and nation, for the final deliverance of our fallen nature from the supremacy of sin and the dominion of the curse. And the more clearly that we see this, with the deeper emotion shall we be able to join in the great doxology which the contemplation of God's dealings with the world through Israel, brought from the lips of the Apostle Paul: —

"O the depth of the riches both of the wisdom and the knowledge of God! How unsearchable are his judgments, and his ways past tracing out! For of Him, and through Him, and unto Him, are all things. To Him be the glory forever. Amen."

www.ingramcontent.com/pod-product-compliance
Lightning Source LLC
Chambersburg PA
CBHW032105220426
43664CB00008B/1141